Keeping on Course

Golf Tips on Avoiding the Sandtraps of Today's Business World

Keeping on Course

GOLF TIPS ON AVOIDING THE SANDTRAPS OF TODAY'S BUSINESS WORLD

GARY SHEMANO

WITH

ART SPANDER

McGraw-Hill

NEW YORK   SAN FRANCISCO   WASHINGTON, D.C.   AUCKLAND   BOGOTA
CARACAS   LISBON   LONDON   MADRID   MEXICO CITY   MILAN
MONTREAL   NEW DELHI   SAN JUAN   SINGAPORE   SYDNEY   TOKYO   TORONTO

McGraw-Hill

A Division of The **McGraw·Hill** *Companies*

Another book from Affinity Communications Corporation

Copyright © 1997 by Affinity Communications Corporation. All rights reserved. Printed in the United States of America. Except as permitted under the United States Copyright Act of 1976, no part of this publication may be reproduced or distributed in any form or by any means, or stored in a database or retrieval system, without the prior written permission of the publisher.

1 2 3 4 5 6 7 8 9 0   DOC/DOC   9 0 2 1 0 9 8 7

Library of Congress Cataloging-in-Publication Data
Keeping on Course
160p. cm

ISBN 0-07-001628-3
1. Business   2. Sports—Golf

Printed and bound by R. R. Donnelley and Sons, Inc.

McGraw-Hill books are available at special quantity discounts to use as premiums and sales promotions or for use in corporate training programs. For more information, please write to the Director of Special Sales, McGraw-Hill, Inc., 11 West 19th Street, New York, NY 10011, or contact your local bookstore.

This book is printed on recycled, acid-free paper containing a minimum of 50% recycled, de-inked fiber.

Designer: Shawnee Slawson

Gary Shemano's proceeds from the sale of this book will be donated to charity.

Table of Contents

FOREWORD

The game of golf is quite astounding—it's truly more than just a game. Unlike most other sports, team or individual, the golfer's experience and goals truly transcend the mere hitting of a little white ball. For those who understand the game on all its levels, it certainly is reminiscent of life itself. As golf resembles life, its parallels to business are quite remarkable. Many of the business people I have encountered talk about these parallels incessantly. Sometimes sportswriters or business columnists will write about this unique aspect of golf, but more often than not they miss the mark by failing to appreciate the deep rooted truths to the parallels.

Gary's book takes the high road and puts golf and what it stands for on a very traditional level. Remarkably, Gary has been able to take the concept of golf, which on the surface seems simple enough, and expose its complexities and subtleties as they relate to business in an enjoyable and amusing format. Reading this book will offer everyone an insight into "the game" a bit better, whether that "game" is golf, business, or life.

—Ken Venturi, Golf Commentator, CBS Sports
Winner, 1964 U.S. Open

ACKNOWLEDGEMENTS

Many people contributed directly and indirectly to the sum and substance of this book, and without them it never would have come to fruition. First, many thanks to all my golf mentors and friends, including but not limited to George Archer, Bud Brody, Roger Cleveland, Johnny Miller, Ken Venturi, and Woody Wright. Second, thanks to George Roberts and the many businesspeople, too many to name, who over the years have showed me the way, offered me their trust, and extended their friendship. To Stephen Mittel who gave me my first trade and whose wisdom has carried me through difficult times, my everlasting thanks.

Also, my thanks to Howard Cohl who believed I had something worth saying, and to Art Spander for helping me say it. To Julie Lueras, thanks for your patience and understanding. Finally, and above all, this book is a legacy to my two sons, Ben and Jake, and dedicated to Jake and Rhoda, who were as remarkable as people as they were as parents.

How it all began

They call it the American Dream, but it should be called the American Reality. My grandfather was living in Mogolov, Russia, when he read somewhere that there was gold in the streets of San Francisco. It was a misinterpretation—there was a narrow thoroughfare named Gold Street. In 1917, with the Russian Revolution under way, my grandfather started toward California. He went east, not west, to Kobe, Japan, before finally emigrating to San Francisco. Soon he sent for his wife, daughter, and son (my father, Jake, who was two years old at the time), and got a job as a barber.

Taking advantage of an opportunity he never would have known in the old country, my father worked his way through San Francisco State University. While a student there, he would occasionally pass by one of the golf courses in that area of the city. He loved the beauty. He also understood that being able to play golf increased a person's social status. So when he eventually achieved a somewhat comfortable level of success as a banker, he took up the game, playing at one of San

Francisco's historic municipal courses, Lincoln Park, out past the Golden Gate Bridge.

My older brother Richard would join my father on weekends at Lincoln, and I would tag along, maybe putting a few times before they walked to the next tee. That was my introduction to golf, and my love of the game became forever entwined with the love of my family. As our economic lot improved, my father joined the Lake Merced Golf Club in San Francisco, where my mother took up golf in order to spend time with the family. And that's where I began to play, at age 10.

I started taking golf seriously in my early teens. Little did I realize how dramatically my life would be altered by my passion for this game. By my senior year in high school, I was beating the likes of those destined to become great PGA champions, like Johnny Miller and Bobby Lunn. I was accepted into the University of Southern California on the strength of my game. While at USC, I learned what dedication and competition really meant. More importantly, I learned how to apply what I learned playing golf to my life and my future.

Following my graduation from USC, I had a decision to make which, in truth, was not very difficult: Should I turn pro or get a real job? Contrary to popular belief, a career as a pro golfer is not very rewarding, financially or otherwise, except for a few elite players. Sure, we read about Tiger Woods, Jack Nicklaus, Arnold Palmer, and Greg Norman, but we do not read about the scores of Ron Cerrudos and Ray Leaches, young golfers with the desire and talent, but not that extra edge that brings out greatness. The Cerrudos and the Leaches are the standards. Recognizing this, and possessing an entrepreneurial spirit that was instilled in me by my father and grandfather, I sought to make my mark in the securities business. Golf became my outlet, my barometer, my entre, and perhaps both my best friend and worst enemy.

While I have not accomplished all that I've intended at my present age of 51 (who has?), I don't look back with any regrets (except the opening tee shot I blocked dead right in the 1989 British Amateur at Royal Birkdale!). After a very enjoyable career as a General Partner and Managing Director at Bear, Stearns & Co. in San Francisco, I decided to test my entrepreneurial spirit and start my own company—The Shemano Group.

Today, I believe that who I am and what I've done are the result of two things: what I learned from my father, and what I learned from others I have met through golf. I'm thankful that I've had the good fortune to have loving parents, caring friends, and trustworthy colleagues.

INTRODUCTION

*G*olf has been called the science of a lifetime, in which a man may exhaust himself but never his subject. It is a game of skill, but more than that a game of integrity. Character is essential. One plays by the rules or one doesn't play golf. Business, too, has been called a science of a lifetime, although ironically, it seems that the more one learns, the less one seems to know.

Gary Shemano has been remarkably successful at golf and business because he understands both require dedication and perspective. Golf is said to be a microcosm of life; it may also be a microcosm of business.

An individual who calls a stroke on himself that nobody else sees is someone to be admired. And trusted. We're told you can learn as much about a person in a round of golf as in weeks of business transactions. Nothing could be more true.

Gary has known the rich and famous, bargaining with investment stars, teeing off with links stars. He made a name for himself in the boardroom as the Managing Director of Bear, Stearns & Co., San Francisco. He grew up caddying for Ken Venturi and competing against Johnny Miller, both of whom went on to win the U.S. Open. He came of age as a college teammate of Dave Stockton, and went on to win many renowned amateur tournaments, including the French Amateur, astonishingly at the ripe young age of 44!

Gary has offered putting advice to Willie Mays, and has taken advice from George Roberts of Kohlberg, Kravis & Roberts. "It's okay to play like a dog," Roberts told him when he invited Gary to a golf tournament, "just don't act like one." He has played with Jack Nicklaus and been privy to the conversations of the best and brightest in the brokerage business.

How does refusing to concede a 2-foot putt lead to more sincerity in corporate life? How will habits formed on the practice tee carry over into higher profits? How do you overcome nerves when you're trying to win a major championship or a major contract? The insight gained through years of experience make Gary Shemano an expert on these subjects.

All you have to know about Gary Shemano is that one large room of his office on the 18th floor of a San Francisco high-rise is given to computers, stock tables, and telephones; another has a putting-cup-sized hole dug into a reinforced floor, from which a flagstick from the 9th hole of the 1988 U.S. Amateur at The Homestead protrudes. Nearby is an endless supply of golf balls, and a half a dozen putters (none of which work!).

The best thing about golf is also the worst thing about golf: You are entirely responsible for your score. As a result, golfers are always looking for reasons for their troubles. Who or what can be blamed. They ought to be looking in the mirror. Does the same hold true in the competitive business world? Absolutely!

The tips and insight offered in this book, gleaned from both the golf course and the boardroom, will help you avoid the sandtraps of today's business world.

—Art Spander

Mental Attitude

JACK NICKLAUS AND THE ART OF CONQUERING NEGATIVE THOUGHTS

"Go down there and see what happens," insisted Al Maus, the pro at Almaden Country Club in San Jose. It was 1977, and I was practicing for a qualifying round in the U.S. Amateur at Almaden. As I finished warming up, I saw one of the most familiar faces in golf. Actually, it was one of the most familiar hairstyles in golf, the gray curls of Angelo Argea, Jack's caddy. There's only one "Jack" in golf, of course, and that's Jack Nicklaus. He was on his way to compete in the PGA Championship at Pebble Beach, and now his son, Jackie, like me, was going to try to qualify for the U.S. Amateur. I asked the pro whether I could join them for a practice round and he agreed.

Confidently—but not too confidently—I walked down to the first tee and confronted both of the Nicklauses. I'm sure the thousands of cold calls I had made during my early years as an aspiring stockbroker prepared me for this—what some might call a brazen act of *chutzpah*. Luckily for me, everyone was very cordial and invited me along. Playing with Jack turned out to be one of the biggest thrills of my life and a very educational experience.

I vividly remember addressing the ball on the first tee, with Jack's icy blue eyes staring at me as if he were trying to ascertain exactly what I was made of. My mind raced as I tried to impress him with a "picture perfect swing"—which is not my forte. I can sum up that first shot in one word: disaster. I was worrying too much about impressing Jack instead of thinking about golf. But I settled down quickly enough and began to play my own game. Throughout the course of the day, I had the opportunity to talk with Jack, who is considered by many to have the strongest, most disciplined mind of any golfer in history.

Eliminating negative thoughts is a key to success, whether on the golf course or in the boardroom. Jack's method of eliminating negative thoughts is quite remarkable. "Whenever I get a negative thought," he told me, "I just imagine there's a guillotine in my mind. It drops, it kills off the negative thought and my mind is cleansed. The power of the mind is such that you can put a good swing on the ball without any negative influences."

Negative thoughts have no doubt killed more business ideas than all of the incompetence in the world combined. If you approach a business negatively, believing it won't succeed, in all likelihood it won't. Somehow, the subconscious just takes control. Imagine where the sports apparel business would be today if back in the early 1970s a young Price Waterhouse CPA didn't believe in the potential for manufacturing athletic shoes overseas? One thing is for sure—there would be no Nike.

MAKE YOUR DREAMS COME TRUE

There is no progress without vision. When we're young, we have dreams and aspirations that are often created from advice given by our parents and other role models. We dream about the future and try to project ourselves into situations of success. When I was practicing golf as a boy, I used to picture myself putting to win a major golf tournament, such as the U.S. Open or the Masters. And I was not alone. I hear the pros talk about when they were growing up, hitting putts and telling themselves, "I've got to make this one to beat Hogan by a shot."

There are few better ways to clear the mind and reinforce positive results than by creative visualization. And that's not just for golfers. Once a person is in the proper frame of mind, anything is possible. Most successful real estate developers visualize their projects even before the architect puts pencil to paper. Gary Cohl used to turn off the volume on the television set when he was 10 years old and pretend to do the play-by-play for the Milwaukee Bucks. Today, he's an accomplished sportscaster for an East Coast network affiliate.

While I never made it to the pros, many of my dreams did come true. When I was a senior at Lowell High, I won the San Francisco Prep Golf Championship, beating both Johnny Miller, who would win a U.S. Open, and Bobby Lunn, who would play in the PGA Tour. In my business, I visualized running a large office of a major company, and I eventually met that goal. I also visualized having my own company with my name on the door and an office overlooking San Francisco Bay. I have been fortunate enough to make that a reality, as well.

ACCENTUATE THE POSITIVE

There are just as many proverbs about the frustrations of golf as there are about the frustrations of business. Perhaps it's because neither allows much room for venting that frustration. You can't throw clubs (well, you can but you shouldn't or you might be banned from playing). And you can't throw a contract at some high level manager during negotiations (well, again, you can but you shouldn't or you might end up losing your job).

Bobby Jones said golf is a game of passion that can be explosive or inwardly burning. And the eloquent golf writer Herbert Warren Wind spoke for everyone who's ever picked up a club, from pro to 25-handicapper: "Of all the games man has devised supposedly for his enjoyment, golf is in a class by itself for the anguish it inflicts." Or as Charlie Brown might say in the Peanuts cartoon, "Aaarrgh!" So in order to deal with the guaranteed frustrations, you need to give yourself every possible break. Accentuate the positive and eliminate the negative.

When Ray Floyd won the Masters, he used a 5-wood to approach some of the greens. This is a club that is usually identified with amateurs, but Floyd needed height on his shots to hold Augusta's hard greens. So he pulled his 2-iron from his bag and replaced it with a 5-wood. He eliminated the negative—the inability to hit a low iron—and brought in the positive, that wood in which he had confidence. To hell with what others thought.

In business, it is vitally important to accentuate the positive, because in most businesses, rejection is an everyday occurrence. In 1989 a young, naive start-up company called Cinescape Entertainment sought to produce a novel line of motivational videos, featuring star athletes, that would be distributed free to schools. Seeking corporate sponsorship, they sent out hundreds of proposals. All but one company turned them down. The one that expressed interest was Coca-Cola. While Coke ultimately chose not to fund the venture because of reasons unrelated, the entrepreneurs nevertheless used that initial response from Coke as their confidence springboard to very rewarding careers. If Coke thought their idea was good enough to justify a meeting in Atlanta, that was good enough for them. They truly accentuated the positive. They were young, bright, and full of ideas, and the major player in sports sponsorship reaffirmed to them that their ideas were good. The power of accentuating the positive is truly amazing.

THE POWER OF BELIEF

In my 40 years of playing golf, I've participated in various matches and rounds that have moved me to a higher level. These same kinds of experiences also move the businessperson to a higher plateau. The key word is "belief."

At one time, Keith Mattus was one of the finest Bay Area amateurs. He had a Tiger Woods-like ability to intimidate an opponent mentally. He had won almost everything as a junior, had a magnificent swing, and was remarkably handsome with jet black hair and a splendid wardrobe. His very presence was unnerving.

Mattus showed up at Lake Merced looking for a game one day, and I was asked to play with him. I agreed, feeling a little apprehensive. But as luck would have it, I beat Mattus, and beat him badly. All of a sudden, I realized I had the capabilities of defeating the very best on any given day. Such a feeling does wonders for your confidence. Suddenly, you believe in yourself. You don't get so discouraged by a bad shot or a missed putt. Moreover, once you believe you belong, you really do belong.

Much has been written and said about the importance of one's belief system in business. If someone doesn't believe they belong in the game, then they don't. If someone doesn't believe they ought to be speaking to senior-level executives, then they won't. Conversely, if someone truly believes they are qualified, then they are. That's how magical a belief system is. Who's to say otherwise? Whose thoughts really matter but yours?

JAC Investment Company is a small family-owned real-estate business in the Midwest that made its mark in the early '60s developing small, affordable single-family homes. When the founder's son took over the business at age 19 as a result of his father's illness, he aspired to build multi-family apartment complexes. Everyone, except his mother, told him it couldn't be done—he was either too young, or too inexperienced, or what have you. Unswayed by all the nay-sayers, through unbridled perseverance and belief in his abilities, he pushed. Ultimately, he convinced a savings and loan to finance the development of two duplexes. From duplexes came 4-family apartment buildings. From 4-families came 8-families. From 8-families came 32-families. There was no stopping him.

You Can't Win if You're Not in The Game

As a society, we seem consumed with failure. Sportswriters are always emphasizing losing streaks or three-putts. The biggest financial head-lines seem to occur when the stock market plummets, or when a major company fails. Individually, we are constantly confronted by the "what ifs?" What if I miss the putt? What if the stock falls? What if, what if, what if. Of course, there's one obvious way to avoid the possibility of failure. Don't play. Don't play golf. Don't play the market. But, of course, then you can't win either. No, there must be a better way to deal with the fear of the "what ifs?" Lanny Wadkins, a pro's pro and the '95 U.S. Ryder Cup captain, showed me that way.

Throughout my years of competitive golf, I've seen people who were playing in tournaments get very nervous at critical situations (yours truly included). Some show it more than others. How you deal with that nervousness is usually the difference between choking and succeeding. Lanny Wadkins has a remarkable way of transforming nervousness into a positive perspective. He told me, "All I really want to do is put myself in a position to choke, because if I'm in that position that means I'm in the game, and I might *not* choke."

I think about Lanny when I reminisce about the most meaningful transaction of my early business career—taking public Grand Auto, California's largest retail automotive parts chain. While playing golf one day, I heard that Grand Auto was going to go public through E.F. Hutton. Grand Auto's chairman, Irving Krantzman, was a member of my club, and one with whom I had played a number of rounds. I struggled with whether or not I should call him and pitch the services of the company I had just joined as a rookie, Hornblower, Weeks, Hemphill & Noyes. The "what ifs" were driving me crazy. What if I made a fool of myself? What if we make a mistake? What if we came across poorly? What if, what if, what if?

Finally, I called him. "Irving," I said, "before you make any final decisions, can I ask you as a favor to meet with one of the heads of our corporate finance department?" I wanted to get in the game. My colleague met Irving, and they hit it off. We got in the game, ended up doing the deal, and did a terrific job. That was the beginning of whatever success I've had in business, and it came because I pushed myself to get into the game—and I did so by bringing in the right people who could get the job done.

PRESSURE IS A PRIVILEGE

Too many people get nervous about placing themselves in a position where they have to perform. It shouldn't be that way. Instead, we ought to savor and appreciate the challenges in our lives, whether they're in sports or in business.

It's important to realize that such occasions are opportunities, even though they may seem to be hindrances. Many athletes say that the real enjoyment of playing is the competition, even more than the victory. Just being in the arena is what matters. It's a privilege to come up the 18th fairway and realize that you can win the tournament, or shoot your record round, even though you may not. So few people get the chance to get to that level in the first place that it's a shame not to enjoy the experience.

In 1988, I was entered in U.S. Amateur qualifying at Santa Rosa Country Club. All I could think about were the possibilities—to get into the field, to win, to play in the French and British Amateurs. I came to the 18th tee and told myself, "Okay! This is it. You've always wanted to be in this position. For 35 years you've practiced 3-foot putts, saying, 'This is for the Open. This is for the Masters. This one is for the Amateur.' Now all you have to do is hit a good tee shot here and you'll qualify for the U.S. Amateur." I was finally in a position to make my dream come true.

I hit a great—and a bit lucky—tee shot that caromed off the cart path, but eventually I blew a short putt, sending the qualifying match into a playoff. (The old adage is true, "you drive for show and putt for dough.") Realizing I may never have this chance again, I told myself, "just enjoy the ride." Luck was with me that day after all, as I parred the first extra hole and qualified for the U.S. Amateur! As a result of that tournament, I was able to go on to win the 1989 French Amateur.

In this instance, golf and business are so very much alike. If you have the chance to make the deal or start a business, no matter how large or small, seize the moment. Understand that most people in the world will never be where you are, and never have such an opportunity. Even if you can't pull everything off, you at least had the privilege of being in the pressure cooker. The experience will teach you more than you can imagine.

JINGLERS AND OTHER DISTRACTIONS

There's an observation that the whole idea in life is to worry about the elephants, not the rabbits, because the rabbits can't hurt you. There are always going to be distractions, and you have to learn to deal with them—to focus on the matter at hand.

I had reached the finals of the 1962 San Francisco Prep championship, having knocked off Johnny Miller along the way. Now, for the championship, I was facing Miller's teammate from Lincoln High, Bobby Lunn. Through 18 holes of match play we were even. So it was on to extra holes.

Both of us parred the first. The second was a 240-yard par-three— Bobby's tee shot was short of the green, mine came to rest on the fringe. Bobby made a bad chip, lagged close to the hole, and I conceded the putt for a bogey four. All I had to do was get up and down to become City Champion. At that moment, the fun began. I marked, cleaned, and replaced the ball and then lined up the big putt. But I heard coins jingling in somebody's pocket, and I started to get upset. I backed away from the ball, and the jingling stopped. But when I stepped up again, the jingling started again. So I backed away a second time. And the routine repeated itself. The third time I got ready, I heard more noise than just coins rattling. My coach Graham Knox had tackled the jingler, who was the father of another Lincoln High player, and the two were wrestling on the ground. When they finally stopped, I made what was then the biggest putt of my life.

In business, we all have distractions, ranging from incessant phone ringing to personnel problems. To overcome those distractions, you've got to tackle the elephants quickly and ignore the rabbits. That way you're not held captive by the distractions that can sabotage your success. If you don't learn to cope with all the little problems that are inevitable, you'll never get anything accomplished.

In this context, one of the greatest problems businesspeople face is time management, and in particular, managing their paper flow. Unfortunately, that talk about the "paper-less" office is just that, talk. The publisher of *Time and Information Management That Really Works!,* offers this piece of advice: If you touch a piece of paper more than once, you've touched it too many times.

$\mathcal{I}$MAGE

IMAGE COUNTS

There are many truths and untruths in life, but one truth is certain—image counts! It makes a difference on the golf course and it makes a difference in the boardroom. In fact, it's not too far off base to suggest that image often separates the world's successful people from those less so.

It's incredibly important to be sportsmanlike and dignified in whatever we do—whether on the course or in the office. You'll never see a Tour golfer perform a "chicken dance" after sinking a putt or taunt another player after that player performed poorly. You'll also never see a professional golfer who isn't well dressed. Golfers have long been admired for their sense of casual style. In fact, if you're confused about how to dress at the office on "Casual Friday," just watch a golf tournament. You won't find any torn jeans or T-shirts with silly messages—you will find fashionable sportswear in the best of taste.

Countless variables affect your image. Your mannerisms, the way you walk, the way you stand, talk, eat, and interact, and the way you dress and groom yourself all send powerful messages about who you are. As

Mark Weber, the vice chairman of Phillips-Van Heusen is fond of saying, "image doesn't make the person, it *is* the person."

YOU CAN PLAY LIKE A DOG, BUT DON'T ACT LIKE ONE

The business world knows George Roberts as one of the partners of the leverage buyout firm, Kohlberg, Kravis, Roberts, Inc., or KKR, which has controlled R.J.R. Nabisco, Duracell, Safeway, Spalding, K-III, and other companies. I know him as a wonderful golfing buddy, and a class act. George called me one day and asked me to be his partner in the Invitational at the San Francisco Club, a fantastic course out on the western edge of the city. I was in a slump, and I didn't want to embarrass him with my golf. "I'm playing like a dog," I told him. But George understood what was important. He came right back and said, "That's okay, as long as you don't act like one." What a classic phrase! It reminded me of something my father used to tell me when I was growing up: The way you conduct yourself on a golf course will tell others more about you than the scores you shoot.

In business, as in golf, behavior is very important, and that doesn't just apply merely to completing a deal, or a specific stock order. Rather, it defines your character. If something goes wrong, do you throw your pen across the room (the way some players throw their clubs)? Or do you snarl at your clients?

During my tenure at Bear, Stearns & Co., the way we conducted ourselves was a priority of management, a mandate coming directly from Chairman of the Board Ace Greenberg. For example, like all of the firms, we often tried to hire top brokers away from our competition. However, we would only do it the proper way, without paying what is called "up front money." We wanted those joining our firm to know that we played the game by the rules.

I once recruited a very substantial broker away from another company, and some of our competitors called our company "a bunch of gunslingers." But we were quite the contrary. We told the young man he would learn what was right and be rewarded by the entrepreneurial spirit in the organization. He joined us, and subsequently moved to our headquarters in New York. Within a short amount of time, he became a member of the board of directors, created an entire department, and is now an extraordinarily wealthy young man.

TALK WITH YOUR SWING

I've met so many people who talk a great game but play a lesser one. I'm thinking primarily of golf, but it's also true in business. Golf is an absolute sport, of course, so a person's skill or lack of it is as clear as his or her handicap. You might be able to fool some of the people some of the time, but not if you're playing from the blue tees.

I make it a practice never to brag about my golfing, because just about the time you think you have it, you don't. If you ever want to know just how quickly the golfing roller coaster can descend, study Tom Watson, who, in the 1975 U.S. Open at Medinah, shot a 135 for the first two rounds, and a 155 for the second two rounds. So no golfer worth a damn would dare challenge the gods by bragging that he's conquered the game. Those fickle gods who watch over the links have their own way of evening out the score. It remains to be seen how or whether they'll cast their power over Tiger Woods.

In business, rest assured that anybody who boasts continually about profits or sales probably has neither. If you are successful, your successes will speak for themselves. You won't have to run around telling people what should be obvious. Maybe all of this emoting is just a part of the 1990s, but I've always believed that people should tell *you* that you're doing a good job; you shouldn't be telling *them*. I stopped meeting with a close friend of more than 25 years because every time I saw him he would talk about all of the multimillion dollar deals he was doing. By the sound of it, you'd think he was responsible for every deal in America. How much was hot air, and how much was a sense of inferiority I'll never know. I'd rather just go play golf than speculate too long about it.

IF YOU'RE A BAD GUY, YOU'RE A BAD GUY

I've met many successful golfers and many successful businesspeople, and from both groups I've drawn one conclusion: Those who are antagonistic and pompous, no matter what their achievements, will always be considered bad people. It doesn't matter how many clubs you've swung for U.S. Open titles, or how many deals you've swung for hundreds of thousands of dollars. Those with chips on their shoulders end up with a hostility that encompasses them, overshadowing whatever other virtues they may possess.

I spent time with Lee Trevino during the 1996 Transamerica Championships, the Senior PGA Tour event at Silverado Country Club in California's Napa Valley. Walking along during a Pro-Am, we started sharing stories. I found out that Lee used to be one of the more adversarial persons in golf, contrasting with our current image of a fun-loving individual pitching Cadillacs and picante sauce. Lee confided that during his prime on the regular Tour, when people approached him for an autograph he would ball up the paper and throw it back at them. He would even do this to children. And then he wondered why everyone wanted a piece of him or why they were causing such a fuss! Finally, at the behest of his wife, Claudia, he sought counseling. Through that counseling, Lee learned that *he* was the one who had the problems, not everybody else. The counselor explained to him that the autograph seekers were just vicariously sharing in Trevino's greatness. They were not out to torment him, but to honor him. Lee quickly changed his attitude.

As the event proceeded, I watched Lee stop during his rounds to sign autographs and offer greetings, and I thought about how important it is to be caring and thoughtful. Whether it's the golf business or any other business, our skills are only as good as the personalities that convey them.

Regardless of the type of business, one of the most valuable confidence boosters for a young employee is a word of encouragement or a pat on the back from the boss. Most new employees, excited about embarking on a new career, desire to share in the success of their seniors. Giving an employee a bit of time and attention is a simple and cost-effective way to allow that person to share the success, just as Lee Trevino learned in relation to his fans.

GO OUT OF YOUR WAY

While I was on the golf team at USC from 1963 through 1967, among my golf teammates were Dave Stockton, who later won two PGA Championships and is now a star on the Senior Tour; Sherman Finger, a three-time All-American; Rick Rhoads, now the pro at San Francisco Club; and Roger Cleveland, who formed the Cleveland Classic Golf Club Company, and is now part of the team at Callaway Golf. It's Roger's name you saw on Corey Pavin's cap when Pavin won the U.S. Open in 1995. Roger has always adhered to very high standards. He has accomplished his goals through diligence and drive, and above all, integrity. In fact, I've never heard anyone utter a bad word about him.

At five a.m. on May, 7, 1996, the morning of my 51st birthday, I was awakened by the ringing of my phone. Groggy, I barely got out a "Hello." A voice I'd never heard before said, "Gary, I want to wish you a happy birthday, and I also want to tell you that you and I have something in common." I thanked whoever it was but told him I wasn't quite sure to whom I was speaking. "Well," replied the voice, "I'll put it this way—I won the French Open in the 1950s, and I understand you won the French Amateur in 1989. Since we may be the only Americans to have done that, I wanted to take this opportunity to wish you a happy birthday. This is Byron Nelson calling from Texas."

Nelson, who was 84 that day, won 11 consecutive tournaments and 18 overall in 1945. He had victories at the Masters and the U.S. Open. I told Byron I was shocked and honored to receive his phone call. Then he told me he had a friend of mine next to him—Roger Cleveland. Roger had told Byron, a close friend of his, of our friendship and my love of the game. I'll always be grateful to my old USC teammate for going out of his way for me.

I often tell this story when I speak to young brokers. Many think I'm just dropping names. But those who understand the meaning of the story and are able to apply the lesson have a much better chance of succeeding. Any good salesperson can take an order, but it takes more than that to build a relationship based on confidence and trust. Going out of your way for people, not because you have to but because you want to, is a trait that too few understand.

CELL PHONES ARE GREAT, BUT NOT ON THE GOLF COURSE

We used to believe that the golf course was a haven, a place to escape the problems of work, if only for a few hours. Now, however, many people are bringing those problems with them in the form of cellular phones. Unfortunately, they are ruining the beauty and serenity of the game. Some courses won't even allow golfers to carry a working phone.

Recently, I was trying to qualify for an international event when one of my fellow competitors heard the phone in his bag ringing. At the time, we were both shooting about the same score. On the other end of the phone, his stock broker relayed the disaster *de jour* and this guy became so upset that his game just fell apart. He started calling the broker before almost every other shot. When he missed a 1-foot putt at 13, he picked up his ball, got into his cart and drove away, never to be heard from again.

What could he possibly have done on the course to rectify what was happening in the market? He had lost money, apparently, and then he lost his poise. Without the cell phone, he would have been blissfully ignorant until reaching the clubhouse. There is a very valuable moral to this story: Don't ruin your day over things you can't control. Life is too short.

COACHING

The competition is now called the AT&T Pebble Beach Pro-Am. In Northern California, we wistfully refer to this tournament by its original name, the "Crosby," which is short for The Bing Crosby National Pro-Am. Bing originated this celebrity-professional tournament when he and some pals gathered at Rancho Santa Fe, near San Diego, California, back in the late 1930s. After World War II, the event was moved north to the Monterey Peninsula, to Pebble Beach, and then to Cypress Point, where the combination of great courses and awful winter weather made it a special attraction. And it still is, even two decades after Bing's death. For an amateur of any given skill or fame to be invited to the Crosby (the AT&T) is often the culmination of his golfing dreams.

One of the Crosby hopefuls was San Francisco businessman Bob Lurie. A superb golfer, Bob is also a delightful and successful person. (The joke around San Francisco is that while growing up, Bob played with blocks, city blocks.) He owned the San Francisco Giants from 1976 through 1992, but is also recognized for his links skills. Off the course, Bob is as easygoing and polite as anyone I know, but when he golfs, his personality changes. He hates to lose. People sometimes misconstrue his intensity for unfriendliness, but they're simply overlooking his determination and singlemindedness.

Since Bob is a true Northern Californian, he was always dreaming of an invitation to the Crosby. One day he got one. He just couldn't wait to work on his game, because he was terrified of looking bad. We went out early one Saturday at Lake Merced and I said to him, "Tell you what. I'm going to get you ready for the Crosby." He was delighted.

Knowing how much he hated to lose, we went out, two or three days a week. He was grinding to play well and to beat me. He would spend hours in the practice bunkers hitting sand shots. And it all worked. With assistant pro Doug Talley caddying, Bob made the cut for the amateur teams and got to the Sunday round, garnering some TV time. I felt I was partly involved in his coup. And I guess I was, having pushed Bob to succeed in the weeks prior to the tournament.

Every business ought to encourage a coaching system. To this day, at The Shemano Group, the senior executives and I spend time each week going over different aspects of our deals with the younger executives, and coaching them through some of their own deals. Finding the time to coach is not only rewarding for the "player," but it is, perhaps, even more rewarding and instructive for the coach.

THE GREAT HUMBLER

If there is any single notion that golf and business have in common, it is that both are great humblers. In the 1990 Masters, Mike Donald shot a 64 in the first round, and an 82 in the second. *That* is humbling. Securities player Michael Milken went from the top of the financial world to prison. Now the Milken Family Foundation is one of the most charitable institutions in existence—a testament to the humbling yet positive effect of Milken's denouement.

As far as the humbling aspect of golf is concerned, nothing quite compares to George Bayer's play on the 14th hole at the Lake Merced Club nearly 30 years ago. At the time, George was a competitor in the same class as Ben Hogan, Gene Littler, and Ken Venturi, and at 6'6" was the longest hitter on the Tour. George liked to play for money, even with his friends, and he took those "casual" games very seriously. This particular round was no exception. With the competition becoming intense, George found himself on the 14th hole, two feet away from the cup for birdie. He missed the putt, and, in utter frustration, slammed his putter into the green, taking out a two foot divot in the process. Realizing what he had done, George literally fell to his knees and, in tears, tended to the damaged green for 20 minutes. George was so humiliated that he never again showed his face at that club.

PRIORITIES

How About a Manicure?

The late Gene Klein said the difference between owning the San Diego Chargers and owning a stable of race horses (Klein's horse won the Kentucky Derby in 1988) was that the horses didn't always ask to have their contracts renegotiated. Gene was an entrepreneur of major proportions. He was the first Volvo dealer in California, back in the early 1950s. Eventually, he took control of National Theatre & Television Inc., which he renamed National General and sold for $600 million in 1973. He always believed that money would return to its rightful owner. His son, Michael Klein, has met with great success in his own right, and went on to establish his own investment company, Klein-Iococca. Although Michael has been a friend of mine for 15 years, our priorities are not always the same.

Michael belongs to the Hillcrest Country Club in L.A., where Jack Benny, George Burns, and George Jessel not only played but had some of the most uproarious lunches in history. When I was at USC, Hillcrest was one of our home courses, and when we played we would see Burns and Benny and other leaders in the entertainment industry there. Now that I live in San Francisco, I relish my occasional returns to Hillcrest. It brings back great memories. And when I went out for my first round ever with Michael several years ago, it brought out great golf.

There was pressure on me when we played that day. I knew people had heard about my reputation. I was trying to live up to it, and I guess I did, shooting a 31 on the front side, five under, and then birdying the 10th to go six under. I parred 11 and 12 and played right into the group ahead of us, which included Jack Lemmon's son, Chris. So on the 13th tee we had to wait. I was antsy and excited. Six under with a couple of easy par-fours and a very easy par five coming home. I knew I had a chance to shoot a record round.

Michael suddenly broke my concentration by saying, "You had enough? Let's go get a manicure. I'll treat."

I practically gasped, "Michael! I'm six under par."

He looked at me, gave me the "short neck," and said, "So?"

So we packed our bags and went to the Beverly Hills Hotel for a manicure because golf didn't mean the same to Michael that it did to me. I was still shaking when we went to dinner at Chasen's, the restaurant to the stars. I realized then that every person's definition of what's important is different. I could have shot eight under, but that didn't mean a thing to Michael. It was on to the manicurist and dinner.

In business, the importance of recognizing what's important to all the parties involved cannot be overlooked. This is what successful negotiation is all about—understanding from where the other side is coming. When people don't take the time to appreciate opposing positions, it becomes impossible to reach a win-win resolution.

HAVE PASSION FOR WHAT YOU DO

One of the more exciting lessons that can be taken from golf is to go after everything with enthusiasm. When I was a teenager playing at Lincoln Park, the beautiful municipal park in San Francisco, we used to drive cars up to the practice green after it got dark, turn on the headlights, and putt for money. One of the guys who was always in attendance was George Archer, who would go on to win the 1969 Masters. George didn't have to compete against a group of teenagers; he had nothing to win except a dollar a hole, and since he was already well-known, he had plenty to lose. But that wasn't the way he went about it. He'd be there trying to pick up three or four bucks from the kids, and he was dead serious about it. He had so much confidence in his putting, he would challenge anyone to a round and play with only three clubs; a wedge, a 1-iron, and a putter. Nothing scared him. That's a sign of a person who believes in what he is doing and so enjoys it that he practically wills himself to success.

Pro golfer Tom Lehman, on the other hand, forgot about this aspect of life. He struggled with his golf game for so long that he quit the Pro Tour and settled for a job as golf coach at his alma mater, University of Minnesota. But when the administration told him he also had to rent cross-country skis in the middle of winter and teach that sport, too, he went back and again qualified for the Tour. Not only did he go on to win millions of dollars, but in 1996 he won the British Open.

It is often said that we spend one third of our lives working. So enjoy your work and, more importantly, remember why you enjoy it—especially during the tough times. When the stock market crashed in 1987, many brokers left the industry. At Bear, Stearns & Co., I remember Ace Greenberg, on the nationwide intercom connecting all the offices, urging us to keep sight of the opportunity that awaits, and to remind ourselves why we chose to be in this profession.

HARD CHOICES

Tough choices are a fact of life in whatever you do. How we make those choices defines who we are.

I knew something was wrong when I saw the club pro, John Murray, standing in the middle of the fairway. It was a windy and cold November day at Bodega Bay Golf Course, which is about 50 miles north of San Francisco. I was playing the 9th hole and had a six-shot lead in the North Coast Amateur. When I saw the look on Murray's face, my stomach got queasy. Sure enough, he came up and told me my father had passed away. Obviously, this was a terrible moment in my life. My father—my best friend—had died. He had been ailing, but had insisted that I enter the tournament anyway. I wondered what I should do. Continue, or withdraw immediately and return home?

We've all read about or known people who have suffered grievous losses but just went on. They say they continued their endeavors because their loved ones would have wanted them to do so. But I chose to do the opposite. I would have loved to win the tournament in my father's memory, but

I couldn't go on. I returned to San Francisco with two friends, Bob Grossman and Dr. John Blankfort, who were also playing in the tournament. As we drove back, I thought about how lucky I was to have talked to my father just the day before the tournament began. He was so excited to think that I would be playing, in effect, for him.

Sometimes you make the wrong choice. Sometimes you make the only choice possible. Only the person involved can decide what is right. Sandy Koufax, you may recall, refused to pitch a World Series game that was played on a Jewish High Holiday.

A year later, on the anniversary of my father's death, I went back to Bodega Bay and won the North Coast Amateur. It was one of the emotional high points of my life. Sometimes only hindsight can convince you that you made the right choice.

PASSION AND THE PRESIDENT

A close friend of mine, who happens to be a frustrated golfer, said that if I contributed to the campaign of U.S. Senator Dianne Feinstein (a former mayor of San Francisco) and the Committee to Re-Elect the President, I would be invited to meet President Clinton and Vice President Gore. I did contribute, and was invited to a private reception with Clinton and Gore at the Venetian Room in the Fairmont Hotel in San Francisco.

While waiting my turn to meet the President, I was stunned to see my cousin, Michael Levin. I had forgotten that he was in the Secret Service. Michael personally introduced me to Mr. Clinton and Mr. Gore. I reminded the President that he had played golf at my club, Lake Merced. "How come you never ask me to join you?" I kidded him. I had been Merced club champion ten times. Mr. Clinton said, "Well, I don't know why you haven't played with *me*." I replied, "*You're* the President." When he asked for my card I told him, "You probably have thousands of cards, and you'll misplace it. It won't mean a thing." He shook his head, pointed to his right pocket and said, "No, no, no. Those I want to play golf with, I put their cards in this pocket. The others I just want to stay in touch with, I put their cards in my left pocket."

He put my card in his right pocket. We had our picture taken—and a year and half later, I'm still waiting for the game. I am still getting solicited for donations, though, so I assume I'm now a left pocket guy.

Over the years, my passion for golfing has led me to meet some of the most interesting people in the world, including the President of the United States. And many of those encounters have led to business dealings. It is our passions that drive us to success. If you are not currently following your passions, start now. That is what life is about. The more we follow our passions with energy and vigor, the more remarkable the opportunities that will come our way.

DEFINING THE NORMS

There are a lot of people preaching about how to achieve success. In fact, the "success industry" is now a huge business. And while you have to think positively and believe in yourself, the game of golf will teach you that you also have to be a realist. Hey, balls take bad bounces just as business plans take strange turns. In fact, you'd be hard pressed to find a single entrepreneur who has witnessed a business evolve exactly as planned. After all, three months of a bad market can change a lot of things.

Hale Irwin has a great mental approach to the game, which may be why he won the U.S. Open three times. He says that when most of us go out for a game of golf, we think that playing well is normal and playing badly is an aberration. In truth, it's the other way around. Your normal game is missing two-footers or "chili dipping." Playing well, Hale contends, is the abnormality. That sort of goes along with the assertion by Walter Hagen that of the 70 or 80 or 90 swings you take on a course, maybe only four or five will hit the ball perfectly—and maybe not even that. Once we accept that premise, it becomes much easier to improve, keep at it and keep hustling.

People in business can draw a similar parallel from the unique insights offered by Irwin and Hagen. Remember, it is not the norm in business that every proposal presented gets approved or funded, that every cold call results in a sale, or that every presentation brings in a new client. Rather, it's just the reverse. In fact, generating five leads for every 100 cold calls is an achievement, and if one turns into a client, it's a great success. The direct-mail business functions in much the same way. If one million pieces of mail are sent, and one-half of one percent responds, the campaign is a tremendous success! Imagine that, a situation in which a 99½ percent failure rate is a success.

Knowing the norms in business will make it all the more probable that one can achieve results. In golf, you may ask yourself after a round, "What could I have done better?" In business, it's the same question. Not clinching the deal may be the normal routine, comparable to Hale Irwin's definition of a golf round. So, you just tee it up once more and let it fly. Nothing comes easy, whether it's a lot of birdies or a big contract.

Knowing When to Say When

The day Dave Stockton was told he was getting a scholarship to USC, he went with coach Stan Wood to play Los Angeles Country Club—and shot 90.

But Dave Stockton was as mentally tough as anyone; a great chipper and putter who was never intimidated. The most important lesson I learned from Dave was "When you get into trouble, make sure you don't get into more trouble." The parallel in business is striking. For example, those who invest in the stock market are often tempted to average down (buy more stock as the price decreases) when they see their stock plummeting. If it's a poor company, all they are doing is "getting into more trouble."

Ego and greed often cloud our judgement. This can result in poor decision making and risk taking. When this happens, it's important to recognize it and take a step back to analyze the situation more carefully and rationally. Ask yourself, do you really want to try to hit the ball between that "V" in the tree?

BLUFFING

In business negotiations you often have the opportunity to make your counterpart think you're bringing more to the table than the next guy (or that you know more than the next guy). Bluffing is the appropriate word. Can you bluff in golf, too? Absolutely. I found out the hard way.

I was playing for USC in the Southern California Intercollegiate at Bermuda Dunes, one of the courses in the desert that they use almost every year for the Bob Hope Chrysler Classic Pro Tournament. I was paired with one of my teammates, Lee Davis, with whom I must have played two or three times a week. So I knew his game as well as my own. What I didn't know was that I could be conned.

Lee and I were tied for the lead. You hear all the time that you should think about your own game, not anybody else's. But since I was so familiar with Lee's game, I was watching what he was doing and trying to use that to my advantage. I knew Lee was one club longer than I was—if he hit a 5-iron, I probably would use a 4. When we got up on the tee of a par-three hole, Lee had the honors—he would hit first. I heard him say to his caddy, "Give me a 5-iron." He hit a fine shot in the middle of the green.

"Okay," I thought to myself. "I know what I'll hit." I asked the friend who was caddying for me to give me the 4-iron, and I really struck it well. Whoosh. The ball carried right to the flag . . . then over the flag, over the green and into the yard of a home that borders the course. Out-of-bounds! I was chagrined. If Lee hit a 5 on the green, how could I hit a 4 over? I took a 5-iron, put down a new ball—the penalty is stroke and distance—and hitting three, smacked the ball on the green. Walking toward the hole, I asked Lee what he hit. "6-iron," he answered. "Why that son of a gun," I said under my breath. He knew I was listening when he asked for his club. He bluffed me out of my shoes, and it cost me the tournament. His move was competitive and legal, and at the right time. In the same way, bluffs can be used to your advantage in business. My father, the former president of Golden Gate National Bank, always told me, "You have a head on your shoulders, use it." He said that right.

BEING AGGRESSIVE

I've always admired Arnold Palmer's aggressiveness. One year I was in the finals of my club championship and the match was "dormie." I was two up with two holes to go. I got conservative and hit an iron off the tee of the 17th. I bogeyed and lost the hole. Then I hit a good drive at 18, a par-five, but once more I wanted to be safe. Instead of hitting a fairway wood, I again went to an iron. And again I bogeyed and lost the hole. Then I lost the match in a playoff.

I thought I was being smart. Instead I outsmarted myself. I had been confident and aggressive the entire day, and then with two holes to play, I changed my tactics—pulled in my horns, as it were. I had no one to blame but myself. I blew it. But I learned my lesson.

When asked about doing something differently in a big game, football coaches will say, "Dance with what brung ya." Same thing in golf or business. If you've been aggressive and it's worked, whether on the course or in the office, then you stay aggressive. You don't change when you're about to close a deal or close out an opponent.

The aggressiveness Arnold Palmer has shown on the golf course carries over into his business and personal life as well. Recently, Palmer learned he had prostate cancer. He immediately checked into the Mayo Clinic in Rochester, Minnesota, and investigated several treatment options. Without hesitation he opted for the more aggressive approach—surgery.

"It's like having two trees in front of you and you're about 180 yards from the green with a 5-iron in your hand," he said. "You can pitch it out and then hit a wedge to the green. Or you can hit it between those trees, and if you don't have to hit another shot, you're done. I wanted to be done."

CHANGE TO SOMETHING NEW

Talk to an amateur and invariably he'll tell you he wishes he could play golf every spare moment. Talk to a touring professional, and he'll tell you he wants to do anything but play golf—at least for recreation. This isn't merely an extension of the adage that one man's meat is another's poison.

Instead, it reaffirms the notion that we all need a change, something different. That's why golfers are always looking at new equipment, even a month after they've bought new clubs.

I change the grips on my clubs two or three times a year. Before tournaments, I clean my own clubs, scraping the grooves and shining the faces of the irons. The process helps me feel energized. In business, too, breaking the routine helps employers and employees alike stay focused and spirited. This is, no doubt one of the reasons why "casual Friday" has become so popular and common in today's offices. According to a recent *Daily News Record* survey, 70 percent of those surveyed indicated that they can wear casual clothes to work, and scores of other studies indicate a correlation between the occasional relaxed atmosphere and a boost in general office morale.

STRATEGY ON PAR-FIVE'S

A par-five, in theory if not in fact, is a golf hole that calls for three shots to reach the green, and then perhaps making the first putt for a birdie. But in truth, many par-fives embody the concept of the heroic challenge, with a lake or a bunker or maybe an inlet of the sea coming into play on the first or second shot. If you have the guts and the game, you try to reach the green in two, and then you're putting for an eagle or, if you two-putt, for a birdie. Of course, if you fail to pull off the shot, you might end up in a hazard, so the possible eagle turns into a bogey—or worse. The two par-fives on the back nine at Augusta National offer heroic challenges. They are relatively short, by today's standards at least—486 yards at 13 and 500 yards at 15—but with water in front of the green. If you hit two great shots, you're on. If you falter, you're in Raes Creek or a pond. Just as in business, you have to know when to be aggressive and also when to be conservative.

In the 1996 Masters, Nick Faldo, who had already won that tournament twice previously, started the final round six shots behind Greg Norman. Nick hit a good drive on the 13th, around the dog leg. But the fairway slopes from right to left, so there's always a question of whether you go for the green, and maybe dump it into the creek, or lay up short and pitch on with your third shot. Faldo debated between a 4-wood and an iron. On television, my old pal Ken Venturi told the CBS audience that the ball was in a difficult lie. When Faldo returned the wood to his bag, the spotter told Venturi, via radio, "Well, it looks like he's going to lay up." But when Faldo started his swing, Venturi told the television viewing audience, "He's not swinging like he's laying up." And to prove Venturi correct, Faldo did no such thing. Instead, using a 2-iron, Faldo landed the ball on the green and made the birdie.

By contrast, three years earlier, Chip Beck came to the 15th in second place, trailing Bernhard Langer by three shots. If he was to have any chance, Beck needed an eagle. Since he was 236 yards from the front of the green and tour pros hit their 3-woods 240 to 250 yards, there shouldn't have been any hesitation about what he would do. But not only did Beck hesitate, he retreated. He laid up with an iron, wedged onto the green and two-putted for a par. He tied for second in a tournament where the only place that counts is first.

Through the years, I've seen many executives who keep looking over a deal but never act. They "lay up" instead of "going for the green."

Others feel that something is right and just go for it. It's always better to try and fail than to sit around for years agonizing over what might have been.

Nevertheless, while no one should allow himself to live in the temple of regret, one must balance the risk versus the reward in any potential action. Taking a chance in a golf tournament is one thing, but gambling your life savings, of course, is something different.

Do you aim at the pin when you have a $500,000 deal on the table? That's when experience becomes so important. It might just be better to go after the fat of the green, to make sure you take a profit instead of a killing. You won't get your eagle, but you won't have ruined your round either.

In the stock market, by way of example, it is always advisable to determine what your objectives are with a stock before buying. Are you in for a long-term investment, or hoping for a short-term hit? Of course, it's common that those looking for the quick hit will see their stocks go down, and all of the sudden these people become long-term investors. Conversely, the short-term investor, seeing a stock go up, will often get a little greedy and elect not to sell as previously planned. Remember, as the saying goes in the securities business, bulls make money; bears make money; pigs get slaughtered.

DECISION-MAKING

While there are no universal truths to guide you through decision making, one general rule that comes close is this: Your first contemplated choice is usually the correct one. If you're debating about whether to swing a 7- or an 8-iron, go with your first thought. As a fallback, if you are genuinely unsure, use the club with which you are most comfortable. If you're not comfortable with either, does it really matter which club you use? Just choose one and go for it.

A mentor of a business colleague used to say, "decision making is easy because there are only two types of decisions; the no-brainers and the ones too close to call. The no-brainers are easy, after all, they are no-brainers. The others, the ones that could go either way, are actually just as easy. Why? Because if the choice is so close, then it really doesn't matter." He then went on to use the example of the book publisher who spent (and wasted) considerable amounts of time deciding whether the leading between the lines should be a point larger or not. By doing so, he took time away from the more relevant and important roles he played as a publisher. The moral of the story is this: make your decision and don't get bogged down in the process. Tomorrow will be another day with new decisions to make.

PRACTICE AND PREPARATION

The Harder You Work, the Luckier You Get

Ace Greenberg used to tell me, "The harder you work, the luckier you get." It's not an original idea, but it's a very true one. I remember playing for the U.S. in the 1981 Maccabiah Games, the so-called Jewish Olympics, at the Caesaria course in Israel. One of my teammates was Corey Pavin, who would eventually turn pro and go on to win the 1995 U.S. Open, along with a ton of other pro tournaments. At Caesaria, Corey spent hours working on what's called a flop shot; a wedge hit almost straight up so it comes down without much of a roll. We got to the 18th hole, and Corey, who needed a par to get into a playoff for the championship, hit his approach over the green. He seemed to have no chance of getting his next shot close to the pin. But then he hit what some called "a miracle shot" and saved par. Except, of course, that the shot wasn't a miracle, and it wasn't luck. It was the same flop shot that he had practiced over and over again. Corey was ready for any possibility.

It's no different in business. If you prepare yourself for every situation, then you'll be ready for whatever comes. For example, when preparing for an impending large-scale negotiation, go through a practice negotiation session with one or two of your colleagues. Have them play the role of the adversary—the tougher the better. Instruct them to ask detailed questions. After all, you never know when that flop shot will come in handy.

KNOWING VERSUS DOING

The difference between hitting balls on the range and hitting them on a course is the difference between night and day. In the first setting, there is no pressure and you can build a tempo through repetition. In the other setting, there's pressure, negative input and usually more than four hours of swinging and walking, during which your tempo may change many times. So instead of going to the practice tee before a round, many pros suggest simply to concentrate on several swing thoughts and then loosen up. Most players find this to be more effective than swinging a lot and disrupting one's game by trying to institute changes.

Similarly, there is a tremendous difference between just reading about deals and actually doing a deal. No doubt the education of reading about deals is helpful, but there is no substitute for real experience.

Knowing and doing are not the same thing. And ultimately, it's the doing that generates results.

Many super salesmen without advanced business degrees are underrated and not given their due respect. Maybe they can't theorize, but boy, can they can sell. And without that person who can sell, it doesn't matter how good of a product or service you have—or how many books you've read on selling strategy.

WORK HARD OR WORK SMART

Some people will go to the practice tee and swing away aimlessly, hitting bucket after bucketful of balls and accomplishing nothing. So it is in business. Some will get to the office at the crack of dawn and appear busy, but at the end of the day will have accomplished very little. A key questions is this: Are you doing busy work or smart work? For example, you can shuffle papers, which is busy work, or you can implement strategic planning, which is smart work.

Most golfers don't have as much time to play as they'd like (myself included). Thus, it's important not only to use practice sessions smartly, but to use office time smartly by focusing on what you can do to accomplish a given goal most efficiently. If your approach shots are off, why go out and bang away with a driver? If you're looking to generate more leads, why are you having lunch alone?

When I was at Bear, Stearns & Co., we had 100 retail brokers working for us in San Francisco. They would constantly send out mailers and research reports. I recall one of my partners asking the brokers, "Are you intending to follow up the mailing or are you just going to wait for the phone to ring?" They thought they were busting their asses by spending all those hours sending out the mailers. Well, that's like a golfer hitting a lot of bad shots on the practice tee. So, we instituted a policy that every mailer had to be followed-up with a call. And their time became much more productive.

PERFECT PRACTICE MAKES PERFECT

Johnny Miller grew up in San Francisco. In fact, we played against each other in the City Golf Championship. John's dad, Larry, got him started in golf by having him hit balls into a canvas screen at home.

Then John started taking lessons from the late John Geertsen Sr., a patient, diligent man who was the pro at San Francisco Golf Club until his retirement.

To get Miller used to feeling the pressure he would face in tournament golf, at the end of every practice session Geertsen would have Johnny step up to a ball and would offer him a hypothetical situation. "Okay, you're behind a tree, and you have to get the ball down in two to tie for the U.S. Open," Geertsen would propose. He would then tell Miller to hit a fade or a hook, or a high shot, or some other unusual shot. And if Miller did not perform, he would have to do it again, to gain experience producing when it mattered. Johnny, of course, would go on to win the 1973 U.S. Open at Oakmont.

A similar comparison can be made between preparing to give a presentation and actually giving the presentation. It's easy to hit practice shots if they don't mean anything, just as it's easy to practice a presentation when no one is listening. But performing in actual situations is not easy at all. It takes smarts and it takes guts. More importantly, it takes proper preparation. Whenever preparing to give a presentation, if you don't put yourself in an actual game-like situation (meaning, in a conference room with people present and interrupting you with questions), you are not taking full advantage (or reaping the full benefits) of your practice sessions.

CATCHING LIGHTNING IN A BOTTLE

I can remember Arnold Palmer saying it doesn't take much to go into a slump, maybe just one bad swing, but it takes a long time to pull out of one. Mastering golf is like catching lightning in a bottle. And it's not uncommon to think that just when it seems like the bottle is capped, it escapes. Or conversely, just when it seems like it is time to give up the game, bang—you rebound. In the 1997 AT&T tournament at Pebble Beach, Tiger Woods shot 70 and 72 on the first two rounds, and then amazingly shot a 63 and a 64 on the last two rounds. He ended up losing by one stroke to Mark O'Meara, who shot four 67s.

The same impulse that drives the golfer's quest to master the game is what makes successful businesspeople keep searching for that next deal. The people who say, "Why would Wayne Huizenga want to build another company, an auto retail business, no less?" do not appreciate the emotional aspects of such a challenge. The challenge Huizenga faces with AutoNation is nothing short of Herculean. It is not, in all cases, the money that businesspeople are after, but the mastering of an art. Business, too, is like catching lightning in a bottle.

PARALYSIS BY ANALYSIS

I often meet people who have 10 corporations formed and have 10 different ways of running them. They seem a lot more concerned with the structure of their business than with the substance of their business. They analyze everything, but they never understand that the essence of business is to generate revenue. Or, as the old golf saying goes, when somebody one-putts, chips in, or bounces one off a tree onto the green, "It ain't how, it's how many."

Projection is not as important as implementation. You have to manufacture a product, or projection doesn't mean a thing. Then you have to sell it, or projection is still meaningless. Chuck Hogan, a wonderful teacher, says that in golf you can't see the target when you're thinking of technique. Again, "it ain't how, it's how many." At some point you have to forget all about grip or stance and just let your instincts take over and swing away.

When I was growing up, a man named Ed Castagnetto would practice at our club. He was good enough to win the San Francisco City tourney. He was also the finest iron player I've ever seen. On the range, he would hit every shot with a draw, right to left. He just had one problem. Out on the course, he tried to hit everything with a cut, left to right. He never went with what was natural. He dissected his swing and had so many ideas going through his mind that many times he couldn't perform in competition.

In business, so many times we negotiate against ourselves, which, like in golf, leads to "paralysis by analysis." One successful entrepreneur was just about to close a $2 million dollar deal when he began to over-analyze it. A friend of his played a key role in the deal as a finder. The entrepreneur had thought long and hard about how much to pay his friend. At first he thought 10 percent was a fair amount. After all, how could the friend complain about receiving $200,000 for putting two people together? But after a while, the entrepreneur thought, "Boy, if it weren't for him I would never have had the deal." So, he decided to up his colleague's cut to 50 percent. But then he began to think, "Boy, this will really set my career, and I owe it all to my friend. Even if I receive $500,000, that will be fine." So he decided to give his friend 75 percent of the deal. The next day the two were taking on the phone. The entrepreneur was nervous because he kept thinking that maybe keeping $500,000 was too much. So, he decided the best thing to do was to ask his friend what he thought was a fair commission.

"I've always wanted a Harley," the friend responded.

DEALING WITH THE YIPS

The "yips" is a nervous, herky-jerky, no-confidence putting stroke. I've had it for more years than I choose to remember. And like a serious disease, the yips grow more virulent with time. No one really understands why or how it comes about. On a practice green we can putt with the best—a stroke that's smooth and flowing. But on a course, in competition, it's as if the putter explodes in our hands, or has a mind of its own. Instead of being in control, we merely hang on.

Bernhard Langer, the two-time Masters champion, has the yips. Or at least he had them until he began grabbing the putter like you would a squirming boa constrictor, with his left hand on the grip and his right hand wrapped around his left forearm. I remember watching Langer on television. He had about a six or seven-footer and actually knocked the ball off the green into a bunker. I asked myself, "How the hell can that happen?" Twelve years later I found out. It was the yips.

Having studied the yips out of my own desperation, I've concluded that they come from a combination of bad vision and a subconscious fear of success. Dr. Cary Middlecoff, a dentist who played the Tour, once said, "You have 2,000 two-foot putts in your bag for your career. And once they're gone, you should retire." Strong words, but there may be a germ of truth.

In 1989, I entered the French Amateur, almost against my better judgment. I wasn't playing well, wasn't putting well, and was under emotional stress. When I arrived at the course, *Golf de Morfontaine,* I put on a large-brimmed cap so nobody could see my face and started putting with my eyes closed. I did it for the entire week. With the heavy Anvil putter I used, I was able to stroke the ball without flinching because I didn't know when contact would be made. It was a brilliant stopgap measure—but only that.

After three weeks, when I began to peak, I started thinking of something Johnny Miller told me. He said when you find something new that works, whether it's a club or a swing gimmick, you have to make sure it's not a "Woweye," or a "one-week wonder." I can't tell you whether putting with my eyes closed was a "Woweye," but it was good enough to help me win the French Amateur, and that's really all that counts.

By analogy to business, the yips are very much a part of the cold calling process, a right of passage that every broker must go through on his or her way to building a clientele. You make that call, and all of the sudden when it comes time to ask for the order, here comes that nervous, herky-jerky, no-confidence tone of voice. Fortunately, overcoming the yips in business is much easier than it is in golf. Practice, practice, practice, and call, call, call.

A SWING IS A SWING IS A SWING

One of the reasons Fred Couples is such a great golfer is because his swing is so smooth that it appears as if he's hardly trying. But look at the many different swings of the golfers on the Tour. Paul Azinger, who has an unusual grip, said if he cared about the way he looked, he would have changed it. Ed Fiori has such an awkward grip that people say it looks like two crabs mating. But he wins! What do they care about how others comment on their style? And before Azinger was struck with cancer and underwent chemotherapy, he played well enough to win the PGA Championship. If a swing works for you, that's all that matters.

The same holds true in business. Use what works. If you're the type of person that is highly productive during the early hours of the morning, then arrive at the office early. If you perform better by arriving a little later, then that's when you should arrive. Too often in business, people do things out of fear of what others may think. For example, young associates, in particular, often think, "If I'm not the first one in the office, management will think I don't care, or don't work hard." Let your performance speak for itself.

PREPARATION FOR A MAJOR EVENT

Remember all that contradictory advice you received about preparing for final exams? Some people probably told you it was better not to change your routine, to study as you usually did. Others advised you to take extra time, to guard against any chance of an oversight. Then you advanced to the real world. Suddenly, you were thrust into a make-or-break situation. Should you make a bid for company X? How should you prepare a witness for a trial? Should you go about it as you've gone about your other deals or cases you've handled in the past?

Golfers face the same dilemma when preparing for a tournament. Should they continue practicing as they normally do or should they step up the pace? When I played the French Amateur, I was told that the more practice rounds I played, the more comfortable I would be with the variety of shots that were required. But another player told me that the less he knew about a course, including where the trouble was, the less he would "overthink" about where to hit the ball. Two schools of thought, both equally valid. Through experience, I've found that four practice rounds are just about right for getting ready for a major tournament. Any more or less and the preparation—or lack of it thereof—can be counterproductive. It's up to you to determine what works best for you. This not only applies to matters on the golf course, but those in the office as well.

At one time, we had a very disciplined broker working for us. His two-year plan was to open one new $100,000 account every week, which meant that at the end of this time period he would have roughly 100 new accounts. I've never met anyone quite like him. His day was carefully scheduled, down to when he would go out for a yogurt break. It was like a young Jack Nicklaus plotting a two-year game plan. Needless to say, this broker met and surpassed his goals. After two years, he charted a new goal—to buy a company. Within one year, he found a partner and the two of them did just that.

RULES OF THE GAME

THE NEWSPAPER SCORE

The term "newspaper score," describes a deep-rooted refusal to accept failure. This is a quality found in all successful golfers and business people. You've all seen it: One of the guys you're playing with lags his approach putt about three feet from the hole. Instead of trying to make the next one, he backhands the ball and misses, as if the short putt were automatic, counting it as being made.

I've played golf with many successful executives, and if there's one single characteristic in all of them it's a refusal to acknowledge failure. So after they hit a bad shot, they often take a "Mulligan," rehitting the shot. Or they backhand a putt, acting as though they weren't trying.

These people are so good at the art of business, so much in control, that they can't handle not being in control. I've seen this over and over. I know two entrepreneurs who are so competitive that, even at a time in their lives when they should be relaxing and enjoying the fruits of their labor, they turn their golf matches into wars. It's amusing, and it's also an indication of why they've gone to the top in business.

One is Mervyn Morris, founder of Mervyn's department stores. The other is Stuart Moldaw, founder of Gymboree, Ross Stores, and Athletic Shoe Factory. The two of them are my best of friends. We go to Palm Springs, and each one does anything possible to whip the other guy. If Stu has a newspaper double-bogey six, he doesn't care—as long as Mervyn takes a seven, and vice versa. Why does this occur? Because, successful business people are by their very nature tough competitors. Stuart and Mervyn are two of the toughest.

PLAY BY THE RULES, OR DON'T PLAY AT ALL

If you're not playing by the rules, the game you're playing isn't golf. If you mess around with the numbers on a golf scorecard, you're disqualified. There are no exceptions.

The same goes for business. You conduct business by the law, or you pay the price. And that price often translates into high legal fees, a damaged reputation, lost business, and sometimes criminal charges.

Golf is said to be the only game in which a detailed knowledge of the rules earns a person a reputation for bad sportsmanship. Maybe the person you're with in a foursome doesn't know he can't ground his club in the sand, but it's your obligation to tell him. It was Lennie Clements' obligation to tell Taylor Smith he was using an illegal putter in the Disney World tournament, and Smith was disqualified after apparently tying Tiger Woods for first.

The respect golfers have for the rules is remarkable. Near the end of the 1996 PGA Tour, Mark Calcavecchia called in two days after the end of a tournament to say he had signed an incorrect scorecard. The disqualification may have cost him $10,000, but his integrity was maintained. Others such as Tom Kite and Tom Watson have called penalty shots on themselves that no one else witnessed.

I recall playing in a tournament in New York, paired with a senior executive from one of America's largest brokerage houses. He kept teeing up in front of the markers and I didn't say anything, even though it was a thoroughly competitive environment. But as the day progressed, I noticed that when he hit into the rough, he would stand with one foot immediately behind the ball, pressing down the grass to improve his lie—which is against the rules. He had a pretty good round going, and

I felt a responsibility to protect the field. On 17, he hit into a bunker and proceeded to ground his club before he blasted onto the green.

I addressed him very formally and said, "I'm sorry, but the rules of golf do not allow you to ground a club in a hazard." He looked at me and answered, "Well, this is not a Tour event." I came right back, "No, this isn't, but it is a competitive game of golf, and not only should you know better, but you have to take a penalty stroke." He said that he wouldn't, because he didn't think he had touched the sand, and then he made some uncomplimentary statements about me. So I brought up all the other infractions, stepping on the rough, everything, and when he turned in his scorecard I refused to sign it. He had been an acquaintance of mine, but I haven't heard from him since.

Although sometimes it may be inconvenient, you must play by the rules. In business, it's the same way. As Vince Lombardi said about running plays, "You don't do it right some of the time; you do it right all of the time."

THERE'S NO SUCH THING AS A GIMMEE

In all my years of playing golf, the thing that's mystified me the most is the concept of the "gimmee." That's when someone tells you a short putt is good—usually, if it's "inside the leather," which means between the grip and the blade when the blade is inserted into the hole. This way you don't have to putt the ball, which is a quite a relief for a shaky putter. This is especially true after he's hit, say, two shots on the green and then left a 30-foot approach putt just far enough away so there's a possibility of missing it.

Imagine that Shaquille O'Neal has a layup to win a basketball game, but just as he starts to shoot, he stops and asks Patrick Ewing, "Hey, is this good anyway?" And Patrick responds, "Sure, it's good. Don't bother." And they run down to the other end of the court. Or what if the 49ers had a fourth and goal on the Green Bay Packers' one. Steve Young was about to quarterback sneak, but Reggie White of the Packers yells, "You'll make it anyway, Steve. Just pick up the ball, we'll give you the six points."

Well, that situation occurs in golf thousands of times every day—in amateur golf—and people accept it as normal. One of the great equalizers in golf is that a 2-inch putt is worth the same number of strokes as a 250-yard drive. Before Ben Hogan retired, he could still hit the ball beautifully but had lost his putting touch, and it drove him nuts. "Hitting a golf ball and putting have nothing in common," Hogan once said in an article. "They're two different games. You work all your life to perfect a repeating swing that will get you to the greens, and then you have to try and do something that is totally unrelated. There shouldn't be any cups, just flag sticks."

But there are cups, and so there are gimmees. Why would anyone in a competitive round concede one? Golf is not supposed to include the gimmee, at least in stroke play. The columnist Jim Bishop wrote, "A gimmee is an agreement between two losers who can't putt."

You play as a sportsman, but you play to win. In business you don't make unnecessary concessions, either. While you compromise and negotiate, you don't give away the deal. Similarly, in competitive golf, you don't give away the hole. You make your opponent "finish." When I won the French Amateur in 1989, I was paired in the finals with someone about twenty years my junior. On the 8th hole, in our match play final round of

36 holes, we were both about three feet from the hole, he lying three, and I lying five. He casually looked at me and said "given-given" (meaning yours is good if mine is good). I replied, "No, putt." He looked at me again, saying "given-given?" Again, I said, "No, putt." He missed the putt. And for the rest of the round, he missed every 3-foot putt, and most importantly, the ones that mattered. That was the turning point in the match.

In business, making someone finish is commonly referred to as "crossing the t's and dotting the i's." If you don't cross the t's and dot the i's, rest assured there is a strong likelihood it will come back to haunt you. You can see this time and again in residential real estate. Someone decides they want to add on a room, but they neglect to obtain the proper permits. When it comes time to sell, if the buyer doesn't perform the proper due diligence, he won't realize that the title is clouded. At the end of the day, someone—the one who failed to cross the t's and dot the i's—will have an aggravating and expensive mess with the city planning department.

LEARNING FROM OTHERS

MODELING THE PROS

When I was a young boy caddying at the Lake Merced Club, many of the great players in the Bay Area, and indeed in the country, would come out to play on Friday afternoons. Ken Venturi, who came out of San Francisco's Lincoln High and eventually would go on to win the 1964 U.S. Open, was one of the Friday group. So was E. Harvie Ward, a U.S. and British Amateur champion, Ed Castagnetto and Art Linares, two great local amateurs, and club pros Johnny Fry and Woody Wright, the latter from Lake Merced.

My brother Rich and I would run to the course from school in order to have a chance to caddy for Venturi or Ward—who, in the late 1950s and early 1960s, were as good as any player in the country, including Palmer or Nicklaus. In those days, players didn't turn pro as early as they do now, but this didn't mean a Venturi or Ward didn't have a pro's skill. When these stars were hitting shots, what I remember most was the noise the golf ball made when it came off the clubhead, a sound of power and purpose.

By the time I was a junior golfer at 12 or 13 years old, all I ever tried to do was emulate that sound that Venturi made when iron met golf ball. It was like nothing else I'd ever heard. Nearly forty years later that sound stays with me, a reminder of the way golf should be played. When I'm playing well, the noise of contact and the vision of the ball's flight seem to be one and the same.

I learned by watching Venturi, Ward, and the other golf greats. They were my role models and I used to imitate and even try to improve on their performances. In business, role models are just as important. We can all learn something that we can apply to our careers from just about everyone we meet. I, for one, shall forever be grateful for what I learned from Ace Greenberg about business: "Watch, listen, and learn, and never talk in elevators or bathrooms." In golf or business, one must learn from others.

PLAYING WITH TIGER

We've heard the term "killer instinct" so much in both business and sports that it sometimes seems to have lost its original meaning. What it truly connotes is going after something wholeheartedly, without letting up, until the job is accomplished. It doesn't mean acting like a jerk. You want to make those competing against you look over their shoulders, but not look down their noses. When I think of killer instinct, I think of Tiger Woods—who rose to the pinnacle of the golf world in 1996, appearing on the cover of *Newsweek* for his big tee shots, big contracts, and the big impression he made on everybody. After only nine tournaments, he had already won three, and more than one million dollars in prize money.

I met Tiger at my home club, Lake Merced, during the sectional qualifying for the 1992 Pebble Beach U.S. Open. Tiger was 16 at the time, and stories of his concentration and enormous power were already making the rounds. There was good reason. For a practice round before the qualifying, I arranged to play with Tiger and another fine amateur, Manny Zerman, who had come from South Africa to become a star on the University of Arizona team.

Zerman was planning on making his living playing golf. But I think that simple practice round with Woods affected him—not just that day, but for a long time thereafter. Zerman was just blown away by Tiger's prodigious length and discipline, his distance, and his manner. Manny never recovered. Tiger accomplished the ultimate feat: he beat Zerman by his mere presence.

Those in business can learn much from what happened to Zerman. When you realize that your adversary is a Donald Trump or a Goldman Sachs, there is a chance that mere presence will intimidate you into making a crucial mistake, losing confidence, and not seeking all that you want. All you can do is make sure you're prepared, trust your instincts, play your own game, and refrain from thinking about anyone else's game. If you start to feel intimidated, or you're young and don't have experience to guide you, bring in experienced colleagues, partners, or consultants to help—a valuable lesson I learned when Grand Auto went public.

Tiger, by the way, didn't qualify for that Open. His short game and putting weren't quite ready at the time. Of course, we all know what he's done since.

ARNOLD PALMER

I've had the opportunity to meet with Arnold Palmer six or seven times, and I can truly say that no finer individual or role model ever played the game. Arnie deserves every accolade that has come his way. His diligence and commitment are remarkable. He's never too busy to say hello or to sign an autograph. At a recent Seniors Tournament in Palm Springs, I was on the practice tee next to Arnie. At 64, he was just as intent on finding the elusive secret of a great golf game as a man of 40 years his junior. There was the same intensity, the same obsession. That's the way it is in golf: Our bodies get older, but our mental attitude remains suspended in time. We believe we never change. So it is with Arnie.

Arnie and I talked one day about the meaning of concentration. He said that when you have to remind yourself to concentrate, you're not concentrating. In other words, when you're thinking of what the results may be (say, $150,000 for making a 4-foot putt), you're not thinking of how to *achieve* the result. You are not concentrating.

Having been in the securities industry for all my adult life, I have seen countless stockbrokers pounding away at their "HP 12-C" figuring out what their commission will be on a sale of, for example, 50,000 shares of a given stock. Or how much they'll earn by making a market in a new high-tech stock. They often have to be reminded that the time they are wasting *fantasizing* about the results is taking away from the time spent working to *achieve* those results.

THE IMPORTANCE OF THE CADDY

The caddy was once an integral part of golf and, before the advent of the college golfer, the pro tour was made up of men who learned the game by carrying clubs for someone else. Ben Hogan, Byron Nelson, Gene Sarazen, and so many others started in caddy yards. Now, unfortunately, the caddy has been replaced by the electric cart or, as the British call it, a "buggy." In Great Britain and Ireland, however, golfers still walk and caddies still lug.

One of the great joys of playing in tournaments in Europe, such as the British Amateur, is not just the sense of history one feels just by playing there, but the bond that develops between the player and the caddy. In one year at the British Amateur at Ganton, I was paired with Gary Nicklaus in several practice rounds. Gary is the son of Jack and Barbara Nicklaus, and was using caddy John Sullivan, who had carried for his dad at the British Opens and now carries for Hale Irwin on the Seniors Tour. It was interesting to see the similarities between Jack's and Gary's games, and to understand Gary's thinking. The caddy knew the exact yardages, the strength of the wind, everything. For Gary, it was like having a 15th club in his bag. At one hole Gary started engaging in some negative thinking, and the caddy was an important part of his support system even then. He encouraged Gary to keep in control and play a bit more conservatively.

Good caddies, like good lawyers, accountants, brokers, and consultants, can make a world of difference. In business, consultants are much like caddies. Some offer good advice, and others are not as helpful. Listening to Gary's caddy during that tournament was like witnessing the rapport between a surgeon and his surgical assistant. Just as a good golfer should not necessarily heed the advice of an unproven caddy, the good businessperson must know and trust his or her consultants before counting on their input when making decisions. By surrounding yourself with the best people, you can consider a good consultant a 15th club in your bag.

BEING WITH SAM SNEAD

On the courses at The Homestead, a resort complex in Hot Springs, West Virginia, the legendary Sam Snead became one of the greatest players in history. A golfer with a sweet swing, Snead would win more championships than anyone, taking the Masters, the British Open and the PGA Championship.

I had an opportunity to hear Sam Snead speak in 1988, when the U.S. Amateur was held at The Homestead. One of the things he emphasized was that he'd always pick a player with a great amount of desire and lesser talent over a player with a great amount of talent and lesser desire—the same thing Ace Greenberg used to say about stock brokers.

Tenacity is what it takes to succeed. Along the way, in both golf and business, I've met so many people who wasted their ability because they never made a commitment. They didn't go after things enthusiastically.

Whenever there is a project to complete in our organization, we remind each other to attack it with fervor. Then, if we don't accomplish our initial goal, at least no one can say, 'Well, if we had just tried a little bit harder maybe we would have done it.'" You might have remorse, but you should never have an excuse.

That night, after Snead addressed the tournament contestants, I tossed my camera to a special friend and told her, "Whatever happens, make sure you get a picture of me with Sam!" I pushed my way through the crowd, got up on the dais, and soon I was standing right next to Snead. Laughing, I yelled to my friend, "Take it!" She did, and now when I look at the photo hanging on my office wall I think about what Sam Snead said about desire being more important than talent. It was sheer hustle that got me that picture.

In my business, we get hundreds of résumés each year—and any day of the week I'll hire someone with desire over someone with talent.

LEARNING FROM THE BEST

It's a good idea to associate yourself with people who are wiser and/or more talented than you. In fact, to succeed, it's mandatory. We've heard so often from golfers and nongolfers alike that raising the level of competition helps raise the level of their games. The addition of Tiger Woods to the PGA Tour was a wake-up call to those players who needed the incentive of an extra competitive edge. Many on the Tour realized that if they expected to flourish, they couldn't give less than their best. By emulating those at the top, you can make yourself better.

When I was at the University of Southern California in the early 1960s, all freshman athletes, no matter what their sport, had to live in the Marx Hall dorm. I found out quickly how the greats became that way. It was through a commitment to excellence and an arduous practice regimen. Among those who lived in Marx Hall my freshman year were Mike Garrett; who in 1965 became USC's first Heisman Trophy winner and is now the school's athletic director, and a swimmer named Roy Saari; who went on to earn an Olympic medal. I remember Roy rising early, working out in the pool, coming back for breakfast, going to classes, working out at lunch, grabbing a quick bite, attending more classes, and then going to another training session. And I realized right then and there that if I was going to get anywhere, I would have to become more disciplined, both in pursuing a better golf game and in my education.

I play golf and often talk about success with Joseph Lemieux, chairman and CEO of Owens-Illinois, one of the largest glass companies in the world. He likes to talk about the parallels between a ballerina and a good businessman. Each one seems to glide along almost effortlessly, but behind all that excellence are months and years of struggle, of falling down and getting up again. One must not only make a commitment to succeed, but must also be willing to do what it takes to honor that commitment.

HORSES FOR COURSES

Often when a golfer is referring to either a tricky course or inclement weather, he or she will repeat the phrase, "It's fair for everyone." They mean that everyone has to deal with the same bad conditions, so it's fair. But that's not necessarily so. Sure, everybody in a tournament may have to play in the mud or the rain, but a person who naturally carries the ball longer in the air will have an advantage over one who tends to run the ball onto the greens. A golfer who hits a fade will always have an advantage on a course where the trouble is on the left. A low hitter will have the advantage over a high ball hitter on a windy day. So while it may be "fair" for everyone, it's not necessarily "equal." It's like a phrase used in horse racing—"Horses for courses." Some horses will do better on a muddy track, others on a dry track.

The same holds true in business. People must understand that there are certain times when they'll have the competitive edge, and there will be other times when someone else will have an edge over them. After all, as underscored previously, often what's important is simply being in the game.

Sometimes just sheer determination and common sense can pull you through. But, of course, you have to be a realist. Concentrate on what you do well, while constantly improving in your weaker areas. Scott Simpson always plays U.S. Open courses well because they suit his accuracy. Seve Ballesteros won several Masters, because there, accuracy was less important than length. But this doesn't mean that they don't play on other types of courses.

Selling your strengths and improving on your weaknesses is a proven strategy for success. If oil and gas are your areas of expertise, then concentrate the majority of your business efforts on them. If you're with a small company that can accomplish a task more cost-effectively than its larger competitors, make that a strong point of your selling pitch. Do what you do best. Remember, horses for courses.

ALWAYS BLAME YOURSELF

The best thing about golf is also the worst thing about golf: You are entirely responsible for your score. There are no wide receivers to drop passes or shortstops to boot ground balls. When you hit one into the rough, there's no Brooks Robinson to dive over, pick up the ball and save you from trouble. Because of this, golfers are always looking for reasons for their troubles—when they ought to be looking in the mirror.

This applies to all golfers—not just Sunday hackers. Architects rarely blame their drafting tables, but golfers always seem to be blaming their putters. Or the wind. Or a divot that wasn't replaced. P.G. Wodehouse wrote about a golfer who complained about butterflies flapping in the adjacent fairway. He wasn't exaggerating. In the 1967 Masters, Billy Casper shot a 67 in one round. The next day, same course, same conditions, he shot 75. He said it was because the peaches and sausages he had for breakfast made him ill. Mason Rudolph, a top pro at the time, commented that "Peaches, sausages, and four bogeys would make anyone sick."

Chuck Hogan is one of the most famous and acclaimed sports psychologists in the country. One day I was with Chuck, and I relayed to him the story of my misadventure of taking my caddy's advice as to what club I should hit on the first tee at a major tournament.

Mike Weeden, nicknamed the "whistler," was my caddy at the British Amateur at Royal Birkdale in 1989, and he knew the course like the back of his hand. I was still high from my victory at the French Amateur the previous week, and I had oodles of confidence going into the British Amateur. The first hole at Birkdale, which is where Ian Baker-Finch won the 1991 British Open, is a 448-yard par-four. It has out-of-bounds on the right, trees on the left and a lot of gorse (a prickly shrub) on either side of the fairway. I decided I would use a 1-iron off the first tee, try to save par by getting it up and down and get a sure bogey. (Club members played the hole as a par-five.) During practice, I was making five, and that was okay.

The tournament began, and it was windy and drizzly—not exactly a surprise in England. I was playing with three young Scots who belted it down the middle of the fairway with their drivers. Mike, who had been carrying for me through the practice rounds, said to me, "Laddie, you're as good as them. Hit your driver, not your 1-iron." So I did. And the ball sailed out of bounds, resulting in my scoring a quadruple bogey. I missed qualifying for match play by two shots!

I realized then that "Laddie" (who was in his mid-40s at the time and should have known better) would have been better off if he had just played his own game. Even if I had hit a good drive on one, there was no guarantee I'd make par. I'd made a mistake in believing that the old caddy knew it all.

Chuck asked me how I would have felt if I used the 1-iron and hit it out of bounds. I said not as foolish as I felt when I kept replaying the actual round in my head, millions of times. And I came to the conclusion that if you make your own decisions, it makes the final outcome easier—whether you win or lose. You take the credit. You take the blame.

By the same token, when a deal goes awry, don't blame the lawyers or brokers or bankers (barring malfeasance). You are the one ultimately responsible. Your support staff, be they caddies, psychologists, lawyers, or brokers, are just that—support. Their job is to help you make an *informed* decision, not to make the decision for you.

OF BROKEN TOES AND BAD PUTTERS

I have 108 different putters. None of them work. I've tried numerous different stances, styles, and maneuvers and they still don't work. I was playing with a friend who was putting as badly as I was, and every time he missed a short one he banged the club against his foot. He started limping and finally hobbled back to the clubhouse. His locker was next to that of an orthopedic surgeon, and when he took his shoe off, his toes were black and blue. The doctor checked out the guy's foot, and he had two broken toes. And he still couldn't putt!

Another friend, seeking to "teach his putter a lesson," tied it to his car door and dragged it home. When he arrived, there was nothing on the end of the shaft except a metal stub. He cried when he saw what he had done to his "friend" of 26 years.

One December I was playing at the Las Vegas Country Club and had a great round going. On a par-three I had a 10-footer for a birdie. It sailed past the cup by four feet. Then I missed that one by a foot and then missed again, four-putting. I was so incensed that, like a hammer thrower, I whirled my old Billy Casper Silver Mallet putter around my head and heaved it into the middle of a lake. It bobbed up and down like the periscope on a submarine, mocking me. The air temperature was about 45 degrees, but no matter, I had to get that Silver Mallet back. I took off my shirt, stripped down to my underpants, and waded neck-high into the algae-filled water. With a rake from a sand trap, I finally snagged my own loved and hated old friend of 20 years.

We're supposed to be smarter about things like that. We're supposed to learn in a positive manner, to put our emotions aside. In golf, however, negative emotional experiences sometime become dominant. When it happens in business—and it does—look out. In many heated negotiations, emotions tend to take over and it then can become more difficult to focus on the major issues. The minor personal points soon become all encompassing. If you fear or notice that you are becoming emotionally involved, call in a substitute to pinch hit. Don't let ego get in the way.

In business, wisdom and experience give you a new outlook. In golf, wisdom and experience can sometimes reinforce the old outlook. Would any businessman do anything as ridiculous as grab a contract he's not happy with and throw it in a lake? A seasoned golfer—yours truly—did it with a putter.

WATCH YOUR EGO

Ego should take a backseat to proceedings in both golf or business, but too many times it leaps to the foreground. I've played golf with athletes from other sports—heroes who don't need to brag—but for some reason they think they have to impress you with their handicaps. One case in point is Michael Jordan.

When Jordan came to our club to play, I had to join the gang that was watching him. He took a low handicap. And let me tell you, while he may be the best basketball player ever, a low-digit handicap golfer he is not. The same goes for former New York Giant great, Lawrence Taylor. He may have been "scratch" at linebacker, an all-pro, but he wasn't the two- or three-handicap golfer he claimed to be. Why couldn't they just play to their capabilities and be comfortable with that? Because great athletes can't accept the idea that they're not great at everything.

Bob Melvin, a dear friend, was the catcher for several major league teams including the San Francisco Giants and the Baltimore Orioles. He has always had a lot of golfing talent but doesn't get to play tournament golf that often. One day I was out at Lake Merced with Bob and two other former Giants catchers, Mike Sadek and Bob Brenly. So little old 5'7" me asked them how many strokes they wanted. They wouldn't take any. Their egos wouldn't allow it, and during the round it became a big subject of needling among us.

In business, an ego can really kill a deal. A while back, an acquaintance (I'll call him Jeffrey) phoned me, saying he could arrange casino financing and had put together many deals. He asked if I knew anyone in the market. I didn't, but I put him in contact with a lawyer who represented the type of clients that Jeffrey was seeking. The lawyer and Jeffrey talked, and I later found out from the attorney that Jeffrey had never actually done a casino financing deal. The closest he had come was when he arranged financing for a small office building that was being constructed by a casino conglomerate. The lawyer realized that Jeffrey was, as the saying goes, "all talk and no cattle." Had Jeffrey been up front about what he had done, I'm sure the lawyer would have set up some useful meetings. But as it turned, such was not the case. The two never did business. Ego strikes again.

RECOGNIZING LIMITATIONS

An old adage about the game of golf says that it is a blending of what your ego wants to do, your experience tells you to do, and your nerves allow you to do. Sounds a lot like business. We'd all like to pull off mega-deals and be in a league with Michael Eisner, Henry Silverman, Wayne Huizenga, George Roberts, and Henry Kravis. But do we know what is required? And do we have the guts?

Here's a golf situation: You have a 240-yard carry over water, and as you walk to the ball, you're thinking, "I'm going to take my 3-wood and knock that sucker stiff." But when you think about it, you know you can't hit a ball that far without a perfect swing. And the only way you'll swing perfectly is when you're *not* hitting a 240-yard shot over water—unless you're Tiger Woods or Greg Norman.

Too often, ego gets in the way of making informed decisions. One of the reasons I admire Jack Nicklaus, Raymond Floyd, Greg Norman, and Tiger Woods is that they think like champions. Then, when it's nut-cracking time, they *play* like champions. They know they can pull off the shot that seems impossible. And they also know which shots they *can't* pull off. Donald Trump used to do the same thing in business. He had more nerve than anybody I know when it came to leveraging and putting together an empire. And, by the way, Trump has also played some damn fine golf. He's a single-digit handicapper at Winged Foot in New York, and a few years ago during the AT&T Pro-Am, he had a hole-in-one at Poppy Hills. "The Donald" can swing it.

THE SURE THING

Paul Klapper, a friend of mine, is the closest thing I know to a Damon Runyon character. It's as if he stepped right out of "Guys and Dolls." He founded American International Travel Service, which became the largest company of its kind, and as an entrepreneur he's had more ups and downs than a yo-yo. One day he said to me:

"So you think you're really playing well?" I nodded and told him, "I really am. And the guys I played with today will tell you the same thing." But Paul couldn't let it go at that. Golfers, like business overachievers, often don't know when to say "Enough is enough." So Paul suggested that we make a little deal. If I would give him a stroke on the par-threes, a stroke and a half on the par-fours and two strokes on each of the four par-fives, he would play me on his knees!

I knew that Paul had tried all kinds of crazy shots as a kid, which should have tipped me off. But I also figured that even if I shot par there was no way he could come close to beating me for 9 holes. Not if he was down on his knees.

There must have been 60 people at the club, and all of a sudden they were all egging me on. I'm not a gambler on the course, but some of the guys at the gin rummy table were. Naturally, the whole room came down to watch, and the bets must have amounted to $5,000 that I could whip Klapper. The first thing Paul did was to reach into his golf bag and pull out some rain pants, even though the sun was shining. Sewn into those pants were knee pads. Then he took out a wooden tee that must have been three inches high, and I started to realize that he had done this before.

The first hole is a 430-yard par-four. I got up there and crushed the drive. Paul got down on his knees, teed the ball up high, took a few practice swings and ripped a hook off the tee maybe 230 yards. Unbelievable! Even though I shot even par, I lost.

What a lesson—but in the long run a cheap one. Scams are rampant in today's business world, and even the cleverest people can fall prey. Don't allow overconfidence to misguide you—in or out of the office. One of the more unique business "sure things" of late has been the "Friends Network." Under this program, a four-level pyramid of fifteen people is created: one, two, four, and eight, respectively. The eight on the bottom each make an "unconditional tax-free gift" of $1,500 to number one. The pyramid then splits, with number one leaving the program, and each other person moving up the ladder. It is the job of the remaining fourteen to recruit another eight people who pay $1,500 each to the new number one. In theory the program makes sense, but in practice it is an illegal pyramid scheme. When the group runs out of new investors, those at the bottom of the list, who have paid $1,500 (or more!) are left holding an empty bag.

Often, the only sure thing about a "sure thing" is that someone other than you will prosper.

DON'T LET EGO RULE OVER LOGIC

Is there any way to explain the motivation for some of the misguided things we do, especially when common sense dictates that we shouldn't? It's important to believe in yourself, but you have to be realistic. An 18-handicapper is just not going to break 80, and it's silly for him to expect to do so. In the same way, it's silly for a broker to believe he's going to make millions on a deal that, at the most, may bring in $100,000. But that doesn't stop people from investing in flyers or from thinking they know it all. Nor does it stop people from thinking they can do the impossible on a golf course.

There's a game golfers sometimes play when they're alone in which they hit two balls, and then play the worst shot of the two. In other words, if you hit a 250-yard drive down the middle and a 220-yard drive into the trees, you'd play the one from the trees. And then you'd hit two balls from there, choosing to hit the poorer of those two. It's a great challenge, refines your focus, and keeps your game at its peak, instead of allowing you to get lazy and start to develop bad habits.

When John Brodie came to the Lake Merced Club one day, somebody dared him to play the worst-ball game. Well, John is one of those guys who perks up when somebody tells him something can't be done—especially if there's money riding on the outcome. Brodie said he wasn't ready that day, but he would be back and the bets would be big when he finally showed up.

Without a doubt, John Brodie has to be considered one of the greatest athletes of all time. Unfortunately, because he played in an earlier era, he never received the publicity of today's stars. At Stanford University he was not only a superb golfer, but a quarterback of such skill that the 49ers made him the second overall pick in the 1957 NFL draft. And, of course, he was their starter until the early 1970s. He also went on the PGA Tour while playing pro football, became an amateur again, and after the age of 50 joined the Senior PGA Tour.

We called John "Lefty" because he could throw equally well with either hand. He also loved action. John would wager big money because he had big money. I'll never forget how earnestly John looked at me as he insisted that he never had choked in any situation. He believed that choking happens when you let your ego get in the way. He said that a failure in the clutch wasn't necessarily caused by letting negative thoughts restrict your performance. "Some days you have it," John said, "and some days you don't." While he admitted to becoming excited in tough situations on the gridiron and on the course, he truly believed that he had never "choked."

That's an interesting concept, especially since Johnny Miller and dozens of other pros argue that everybody chokes, the only difference being the better player you become, the higher your choking threshold. It's very difficult to think that your nerves stay the same in different situations and that your play isn't affected.

As I've said, the Lake Merced members were not averse to a little action, but like those who buy blue chip stocks, they wanted to have some indication of what might happen. I could play almost as well as John in those days, so they urged me to play worst-ball and see what I shot. I played well and shot an 88. Since Brodie bet that he could break 80 on his worst ball, I figured wagering against that possibility was like betting the sun would come up in the east.

Rumors circulated that a lot of money was riding on the game, and I was absolutely certain John would lose. When Brodie came down the 9th fairway, everyone walked away—including Brodie. I didn't understand why he didn't go to the 10th tee. The reason was that he'd shot 55 on the front 9 and conceded the bet then and there. The lesson he learned, and one that applies to anyone in business is: Don't take a chance when you don't know what you're getting into. John didn't know, but his ego was such that he felt he could do almost anything—and as a matter of fact, John was such a gifted and natural athlete that he was one of the few who really had the right to believe this. Except, in this case, John could always "talk the talk" and "walk the walk."

In business, you will find that "risks" taken by successful entrepreneurs are very well researched and educated. In other words, entrepreneurs gauge risks realistically. In *David Copperfield,* Charles Dickens' Mr. Micawber was no realist. Although he seemed relentlessly optimistic, Micawber was simply a poor fool who didn't understand the realities before him. (In the same way John Brodie didn't understand the realities of playing "worst ball.") His constantly reiterated hope that something would "turn up" was merely a fool's dream. As in business, well-reasoned predictions are one thing; foolish optimism is another.

PERCEPTION

NOTHING IS AS EASY AS IT LOOKS

The Giants baseball team moved from New York to San Francisco in 1958. Along with them came Willie Mays, arguably the greatest baseball player in history. As a public relations gesture in their early years on the West Coast, the team invited high school players to work out with them and pitch batting practice. I was playing baseball at Lowell High at the time and was lucky enough to be selected. So early one evening, there I was, dressing in the clubhouse of the San Francisco Giants at Candlestick Park!

Soon thereafter, I introduced Willie Mays to my father, who was then the President of Golden Gate National Bank. Back in those days, agents hadn't yet taken over sports, and, as a favor to Mays, my dad helped negotiate his contract. He also advised him on his financial affairs and never charged Willie a cent for his services.

Willie spent time in the bank with my father, and observers began to get the impression that the baseball great was as skilled in business as he was on the field. In truth, this image was created by my father. Still, people believed that Willie was as good at handling tax write-offs as he was at handling outside curves.

My father also introduced Willie to golf, and I'll never forget Willie's first swing at a golf ball. Whiff! His second swing was equally memorable. Whiff! How, he thought, could the game be so difficult? After all, the ball was sitting still! Eventually, Willie built up the grips of his golf clubs to the size of the grips of his baseball bats so that it would feel like he was actually swinging something.

For some reason, many people who excel at one career falsely assume that they can just as easily excel in a different profession without putting in the necessary time; that is, without having to pay their dues. Michael Jordan's foray into baseball is a prime example. Jordan's extraordinary talents on the basketball court simply weren't enough. More recently, a very senior executive at a Fortune 500 company sought an opportunity to host a radio show. Though he had never been on the air, having listened to radio all his life, he thought "how hard could it be?" He knew what he wanted to talk about, and, in fact, his subject matter was interesting and relevant. However, after a three-hour simulation in a studio, his respect for professional radio talent rose dramatically. He was shocked as to how difficult it actually was.

We tend to forget that the things people do well are done well because they have put in a tremendous amount of time and effort. It's almost a universal truth that something that may appear easy only comes easy with effort—sometimes considerable effort. The senior executive so eager to launch a radio show hadn't paid the price of cutting his teeth in the business at small local stations throughout the Midwest. I'm sure someone like Rush Limbaugh would have been equally overwhelmed trying to do *his* job. Willie Mays, by the way, has become a terrific golfer.

KNOW THE PLAYERS FOR WHO THEY ARE, NOT HOW THEY APPEAR

The 1964 U.S. Open champion, Ken Venturi, was born and raised in San Francisco, where his father, once a ship's chandler, became the pro at Harding Park Golf Course. Ken was not anyone's favorite person. He was curt, defensive, and had a stutter, and that speech impediment caused him to become withdrawn and introverted. Venturi once said that his stuttering was a result of his parents trying to make him a right-hander when he was naturally a left-hander. I met Venturi when I was in high school. I caddied for him occasionally, and boy, could he hit a golf ball.

I'm very fortunate to have remained friends with Ken over the years. His unheralded contribution to children's charities was finally acknowledged recently at a March of Dimes dinner. That night, Ken explained to me how hard he had worked to overcome his stuttering. That he succeeded is obvious, since for years he has worked as a CBS announcer at numerous tournaments, including the Masters. So here's a guy we all misunderstood—someone who should have been admired, not condemned. Bill Walton, the basketball great, also struggled to overcome a stuttering disability. Today, he's a top broadcaster for NBC Sports.

Sometimes we form an image of someone without knowing much about them or their circumstances—allowing first impressions to cloud our judgment. We may stereotype all lawyers as being sharks or all stockbrokers as being pushy. You can't do business effectively if you refuse to consider people beyond a superficial level. We thought we knew Ken Venturi, but we really didn't know him at all.

In 1977, one of the most renowned amateur golfers was 17-year-old Billy Corbett. To this day, Corbett holds the course record as an amateur at Spyglass Hill at Pebble Beach with a 67. That year, I was in a best ball tournament at Spyglass and was paired against a team that included Corbett. On the par-three 12th hole, my partner hit his tee shot 30 feet from the cup, Corbett drove about 15 feet, and I lied two about 8 feet. Under the rules of best ball, with my partner being out, I could putt first. But, since my ball was in Corbett's line, I asked him if he wanted to putt. He said no, he wasn't ready. So, I asked him if it was okay if I putted. This cocky kid said no, and proceeded to take a peanut butter sandwich out of his bag, sit on the green, and begin eating! I thought, "What *chutzpah!*", and went ahead and putted. Corbett jumped up and went ballistic. He called me names, threatened to file a protest, and ranted and raved for a good ten minutes. I hoped that was the last I'd ever see of Billy Corbett.

Several years went by, and one day I was heading to my office in San Francisco when I saw a guy selling art in front of the Citicorp Center. I looked at the guy and suddenly realized that it was Corbett! So, I grabbed a picture and pretended to steal it. Corbett raced after me. Then, when he finally recognized me, he asked if I wanted to buy three pictures or four! The kid still had moxie. I invited him up to my office and we began talking. "Listen," I said, "if you can sell this artwork, why can't you sell stocks?" "No one ever gave me a chance," he said. "Well,

I'll give you a chance," I replied. And I did. Today, Billy Corbett is not only a partner of mine at The Shemano Group, but is also one of my closest friends.

WOMEN AND GOLF

To most men who play golf, there's nothing quite as appealing or attractive as a woman in the latest golf attire hitting balls at a range or playing a course. Most single guys who play golf go to the range not only to improve their game, but to improve their social lives. Their ideal woman is someone who enjoys golf as much as they do.

Over the years, however, an interesting phenomenon has occurred. Many men from the "old school" used to believe that business and golf were a man's birthright. But once they began to accept women on the golf course (where many women could play better than they could), they became more accepting of women in the boardroom, too. There is no doubt in my mind that the appeal of women's professional golf has greatly enhanced opportunities for all women in business—whether they play golf or not.

LEARNING ABOUT PEOPLE ON THE GOLF COURSE

Hale Irwin, the three-time U.S. Open winner, said that golf brings out one's assets and liabilities. The longer you play with someone, the more certain you become that his performance is an outward manifestation of who he really thinks he is. Over the years, I've had the good fortune to play with some wonderful people. During the rounds we've played together, I've learned a lot about their strengths and weaknesses (and I don't mean their driving and chipping, either).

Chuck Schwab, who heads his own brokerage house, is a terrific golfer—he's a regular entrant in the Pebble Beach AT&T Pro-Am—and a terrific fellow. In an industry of aggressive individuals, he is remarkably controlled, and a gentleman in every sense of the word. Paul Hazen, chairman of the board of Wells Fargo Bank, who sportswriters dub "mighty mite" (5' 7" at most) has an indomitable spirit. It's no wonder Wells Fargo has done incredibly well under his watch.

I've also had the pleasure of playing with the late Walter Haas Jr., who was not only chairman of Levi Strauss, but for many years was the owner of the Oakland Athletics baseball team. Both businesses were run extremely successfully (the A's won three pennants and the 1990 World Series), and with class, much the same way Walter played golf. Bob Lurie, head of the Lurie Co., and the former owner of the San Francisco Giants, is perhaps the fiercest competitor I've ever known on a golf course. He and his General Manager, Al Rosen (the 1953 American League Most Valuable Player), would always be out there grinding. Bob—"Lefty," as we called him—loved the action.

Chuck Mathewson, chairman of International Gaming Technology, the world's largest manufacturer of slot machines, is at peace with himself when he plays. A very warm and charming guy, he loves the game and just takes in stride all the maddening situations that seem to bother everyone else. On the course he's as methodical and confident as he is in the boardroom. The qualities that make a person so cool under pressure in a round of golf are the same ones that can make him a top-flight businessman. If you want to learn about how someone will operate under pressure, watch him for four hours on a golf course.

ONE PERSON'S MISFORTUNE MAY BE ANOTHER'S OPPORTUNITY

Many people are contrarians or, in stock market lingo, "value play-ers." Value players look for stocks that are down and then buy and wait. They trust management, believing that over time, the company will improve and the stock will rise. They think that another's misfortune will be their golden opportunity. In golf it often works the same way.

How often have we seen a player, seemingly out of the running, come storming back when the leader "knocks one into the drink"? I was play-ing in the 1991 U.S. Amateur at the Honors Course in Chattanooga, Tennessee, one of the most beautiful venues in the world, when Dicky Pride did just that. During the second day of qualifying for match play, I was paired with Dicky. He was playing well, but it was questionable whether he'd get in to match play. The leader in our group was playing extremely well and seemed to be a lock. We came to a par-four on the back 9 with water on the left and rough on the right. The leader hit what seemed like a good shot down the right side, but got a bad bounce into what we call "love grass." In golf, that's tantamount to suicide. Pride, with confidence soaring, duck-hooked his tee shot. Through some stroke of fortune, the ball hit a sprinkler head and, instead of jumping into the water, bounced back onto the fairway. Pride went on to birdie the hole and qualify for the tournament. Following this coup, Dickie Pride went on the PGA Tour and won the 1994 Federal Express St. Jude Classic in Memphis. He certainly took to the courses in Tennessee. And he certainly took advantage of the other golfer's bad luck.

A similar analogy can be drawn from the misfortune that befell real estate speculators in the late 1980s. When the Tax Reform Act of 1986 went into effect, it eliminated many of the tax benefits that had prompted an extraordinary amount of real estate investing. As a result, many speculators and syndicators went bust and were forced to sell off their properties at distressed prices. Individuals with enough ready cash were then able to buy up these valuable properties and capitalize on the others' misfortunes. The message? Don't rule out unforeseen business opportunities that may arise with the onset of a temporary setback.

The Big **Picture**

GOLF IS A MICROCOSM OF BUSINESS AND LIFE

Bobby Jones was as talented with words as he was with clubs. "On the golf course," wrote Jones, "a man may be the dogged victim of inexorable fate, be struck down by an appalling stroke of tragedy, become the hero of an unbelievable melodrama, or the clown in a side-splitting comedy—any of these within a few hours." His words express why golf becomes an addiction. In the four-and-a-half hours it takes to play a typical game, you can experience almost everything possible in life: challenges, euphoria, disappointment, and setbacks. You can even come to an understanding of what is possible and what is not. What it takes to be great in golf is also what it takes to be great in business: discipline, stamina, self-confidence and the ability to overcome problems—especially insecurities.

One of the greatest career hindrances of executives is a sense of insecurity about their abilities. In golf it is no different. And no one can attest to this better than Ken Venturi.

Going into the final round of the 1956 Masters, Ken Venturi, who was an amateur at the time, led veteran Dr. Cary Middlecoff by four strokes. The fact that an amateur lead the field heading into the final round was unprecedented. The entire golfing world was on edge.

Ken was supposed to be paired with Byron Nelson, but because Byron was his teacher, the Masters Committee felt it would be a hollow victory if he won playing with Byron at his side. So the committee gave Ken the choice of playing with anyone he wanted. He chose Sam Snead. His reasoning was that, as an amateur, Ken had played with Hogan, Nelson, but never Snead. He thought, "If I win the Masters, what could be better than to walk up to the 18th green with Sam Snead."

On the first tee, both players greeted each other. Sam, noticing that Ken was extremely nervous, thought it best not to talk to him—which Ken appreciates to this day. In fact, Ken has stated that, if he had to do it all over again, Sam Snead would still be his choice as playing partner.

The pressure of being the first amateur to win the Masters; however, was too much for Ken. Though he hit fifteen greens in regulation, he had six three-putts. With that, he missed out on the unique opportunity to become the first amateur to win the Masters, losing to Jackie Burke, Jr., who made up nine strokes on Ken and shot a 289. Venturi finished second shooting a 290, and Middlecoff finished third, shooting a 291.

To this day, no amateur has won the Masters. To put this in perspective, Tiger Woods, as an amateur with three consecutive U.S. Amateur titles, finished tied for 41st in the only Masters in which he made the cut to the final round (1995).

There comes that point in everyone's career when you must decide whether or not you belong in the game. For a while after that match, Ken thought he didn't belong—even though everyone else did. But after realizing—and appreciating—that in that final round he actually hit 15 greens in regulation, a feat of which any pro would be proud, and that he finished second in one of the most renowned tournaments in the world, Ken Venturi came to the conclusion that he did, in fact, belong in the game.

Quite often, businesspeople recount transitional times in their lives when they finally knew they belonged in their game. A successful real estate developer recalled that when he went to secure his first construction loan at age 18, he was so intimidated by the loan officer that he began to think he should find another line of work. But after a few minutes of conversation, this 18-year-old whiz-kid developer realized that he knew more than the banker. *That's* when he knew then that he belonged in the game.

STOP AND SMELL THE FLOWERS

Walter Hagen, the elegant and skillful golfer of the 1920s and '30s, put all sports into perspective when he said to athletes, "You're only here for a short visit. Don't hurry; don't worry. And be sure to smell the flowers along the way." This advice is essential. Most of us are so focused on our goals that we fail to appreciate the journey we take to get there. And once we reach a goal, we're left asking, "Now what?" Enjoy what you're doing, especially when you're playing golf. We grow old awfully fast. I think of playing against Johnny Miller in the San Francisco High School Championships, and now we're both Seniors.

In 1995 I realized a dream by playing both Pine Valley in New Jersey, and Augusta in Georgia, which some call the two greatest courses in the world. When I was younger, I might have concentrated on trying to shoot a great round at the expense of everything else. Now that I'm in my 50s, I have different priorities. I don't care about "grinding." I care about absorbing every wonderful moment in the dunes and under the pine trees. I may never walk Augusta or Pine Valley again, but I'll always remember the times that I did—and those moments are as important to me as playing a great game.

Sometimes in business we're under such pressure to earn, expand, and succeed, that we forget to stop and understand what really matters in life. We neglect our spouses, fail to spend time with our children as they grow, even forget to thank the people who work with us. I know one executive who prints the notation "Stop and smell the roses" at the top of his daily calendar. Anything you can do to help take a moment here and there to reflect on life *outside* of business pressures and obligations will make you a better person—and probably a healthier one as well.

NOTHING IS CERTAIN

There are all sorts of maxims warning against overconfidence, perhaps the most well-known being, "Don't count your chickens before they've hatched." These maxims exist because it's human nature to think that we can achieve more than we are truly capable. Optimism is an important trait, but it should be tempered by realism. Johnny Miller had a chance to win the Masters in 1971, his third year on the Tour. If I remember correctly, he came to the 15th hole on the final day with the lead. Later he told me, "I started thinking about how good I would look in the green jacket and how proud my father would be of me." Oops—Charles Coody ended up winning the Masters.

In 1981, I made it to the finals of the San Francisco City Amateur, which is called the world's longest tournament, lasting three weeks! "The City" has been won by guys like Ken Venturi (three times), Harvie Ward, and George Archer, but never by Johnny Miller, Tom Watson—or by me. (Interestingly, the 1956 finals of the City paired Venturi against Ward, the two finest amateurs at the time. In front of 10,000 people (one of the largest amateur gallerys in history), Ward shot one under par for 32 holes and lost five and four to Venturi.)

"The City" final is scheduled for 36 holes of match play, and in the afternoon I was two down going in the fourth hole, a 571-yard par-five. I was on in three, and my opponent was on in four. He putted, and when the ball just missed I conceded his next putt for a bogey six. So all I had to do was two-putt from 20 feet for a par to win the hole and close to one down. Sound easy? It never happened.

Through the previous 21 holes, when I was on the lip of the cup, my opponent always told me, "Pick it up." He conceded the little ones. This time I lagged to within two inches, and my opponent walked off the green. Assuming he had conceded the putt, I made a half-hearted backhand swipe, missed, and picked up the ball. At the next tee, he asked me what I had. I told him I thought he had given me the putt, so I won the hole with a five. He didn't. So I lost the hole, because I never holed out. Instead of being one down I was three down. I was so unnerved by the damaging miscommunication with my opponent that I dropped almost every hole from then on, until finally, I was defeated.

What a lesson. You can't take anything for granted. A hole is not won until the ball is in the cup or your opponent tells you, "Good." A business deal is not consummated until the contract is signed. You never take a profit until the stock is sold, no matter what its price in the *Wall Street Journal*. Until the check clears the bank, you haven't finished your business. Bobby Jones said it takes a long while to realize golf is played one stroke at a time. Sometimes that stroke is minuscule, just an inch or two. But it still has to be made.

THE JOY OF CYPRESS POINT

If there was only one more round of golf that I could play in my life, I'd choose to play it at Cypress Point, that wonderful course on the Monterey Peninsula. When Cypress is mentioned, many people think of the famous 16th hole, that 230-yard par-three over an inlet of Monterey Bay, perhaps the most photographed hole in golf. But that hole, as great and challenging as it may be, is only a small fraction of the appeal of Cypress Point. I'm thinking of its trek through the forest, its hike up the sand dunes, its back-to-back par-fives (holes 5 and 6) and its back-to-back par-threes (holes 15 and 16).

The members at Cypress are the bastions of industry, a very elite group. Years ago, during a banquet at Pebble Beach, Bob Hope cracked, "They had a membership drive at Cypress Point, and they were successful. They drove out 20 members." The members at Cypress Point, fortunately, not only have one of the greatest pieces of land but also great senses of humor.

One sunny day, I was playing Cypress, courtesy of J. B. McIntosh, with Gary Schnitzer, of Schnitzer Steel Company, who had long yearned to play there. At hole 16, he hit five balls into the water trying to reach the green, and instead of getting angry, he turned to me and said, "Gary, I think it's just unbelievable there is a group of men so lucky as to be able to play here whenever they want." There's something to be said for his attitude.

Alistair Mackenzie, the architect of Cypress Point, said that the greatest compliment that can be paid to a golf course designer is that the work is natural and not contrived. I think that's the charm of the older golf courses—they fit into the terrain without a lot of bulldozing. Cypress Point has no artificial lakes, no railroad ties, nothing but green beauty.

We all work hard at our chosen careers and it's important to stop and appreciate the wonderful benefits that we can derive from them. For some, it's the ability to play a fine golf course. For others, it's driving a nice car, or being able to travel, or to lie on a beach. Whatever enjoyments you derive from your hard work, take a moment to appreciate them. Don't take them for granted.

MONEY CAN'T BUY HAPPINESS (OR BIRDIES)

Bob Pryt, a dear friend, once worked for me at Bear, Stearns & Co. He wasn't much of a salesman, but he was fantastic as a trader and instinctive investor. In fact, he has become one of the most successful money managers in the United States in the last few years.

Many of Bob's friends and business associates were golfers, and Bob became curious about the game. He wondered why so many executives were enamored with golf, even "possessed" by it. So I took Bob to the Mission Bay driving range on the edge of San Francisco's financial district. I wanted to help him find out what his friends and colleagues already knew; that golf is the most enticing of sports. Bob hit some balls—and hit them quite well. And right away, he couldn't wait to move to the next step.

He wanted to know what kind of clubs he should buy. Now, he had only hit part of a bucket of balls at one driving range, but already he was ready to purchase a set of clubs. So I took him to the pro shop, and they outfitted him with a set of Callaways, the finest clubs money can buy. Bob also bought a full set of Callaways for his wife, Diane, as well.

He went to the range a few more times and I encouraged him to go out on a little par-three course to actually play some golf. But he didn't have the patience, nor did he want to invest the time that becoming a golfer required— even though he had invested a lot of money in two new sets of clubs.

Bob could apply himself and become successful in business, but he couldn't or wouldn't do the same thing to make it in golf. He told me that if he could buy a golf game, he'd love to do it. That reminded me of something Gene Sarazen said to Henry Ford after they'd played together: "It's too bad you can't buy a game off the shelf like engine parts." Those who think that golf is "just a game" are misguided, for golf requires the same dedication people like Henry Ford or Bob Pryt put into their careers. Bob went so far as to ask whether he could hire a golf pro on retainer, spend 15 minutes a day with him and develop a game that would be decent or at least not embarrassing. Sorry, Bob. It doesn't work that way. There are no shortcuts in golf. Nor, as Bob knows so well, in managing money.

ACCEPTING DISAPPOINTMENT

Any references to the Crosby or to the AT&T remind me always to put matters in their proper perspective. Back in 1978, a year after my father passed away, I was tied for first in the North Coast Amateur at Bodega Bay (just north of San Francisco). Bing's son, Nathaniel Crosby, was one of my playing partners. Nathaniel is now an executive with Nicklaus Golf and doesn't play very much, but in 1981 he won the U.S. Amateur. It was a tremendous victory, a gutsy performance against golfers who would shortly go on the PGA Tour.

Nate, his brother, Harry, and his mother, Kathryn, always had a lot of input as to which amateurs would get invited to the Crosby. (The name was changed to AT&T in 1986.) So on the first tee of that North Coast Amateur, I turned to Nate and said, "I think we should have a little side bet for the round." He asked, "What's that?" I replied, "If I beat you, how about an invitation to the Crosby?" "You mean, you've never played in the Crosby?" he responded, and accepted the wager.

As destiny would have it, I not only won the tournament but I beat Nathaniel on the last hole. I was doubly excited, thinking as much about the invitation to the Crosby as I did about my victory.

Well, the months passed, and when I heard the invitations to the Crosby were being sent out, I kept checking my mailbox. Nothing. And when January rolled around, there I was again, watching the tournament on TV. Not long afterward, I ran into Nate, and said, rather sarcastically, "I guess my invitation got lost in the mail." He didn't say a thing. Maybe he was a little embarrassed, or maybe he simply didn't remember our side bet at Bodega Bay. To this day, I've yet to play in that tournament. Of course, I am lucky in one way. I could have been asked to play in 1996 when heavy rains caused the tournament to be called off after two rounds.

Disappointments, of course, are a part of life. We all face them. What matters, however, is how we deal with them, and whether we can put them into proper perspective. The disappointment of not being invited to the Crosby is, of course, trivial. After all, we're talking about golf, not the health of a loved one, or a family's well-being.

The ability to learn from and overcome disappointment is a trait common to most successful buisnesspeople. Tom Monaghan of Domino's

Pizza, for example, struggled through real disappointment before making his pizza chain a success—three near-bankruptcies (including more than one hundred lawsuits filed by fifteen hundred creditors). His secret to overcoming these obstacles was his ability to transform such disappointment into a competitive drive to excel.

SURMOUNTING PREJUDICES

There are golf courses that still do not allow the participation by people of certain ethnicities or religions. And although illegal in practice, there are also businesses that make it difficult for people of certain ethnicities or religions to get involved or move ahead.

There's a golf club I know of in a beautiful serene setting, tucked against a stunning mountain range. But its beauty pales when I consider their restrictive policies. On one occasion, my father, mother, and I were invited to play there. When our host wasn't able to make it because he got sick, we were told that we wouldn't be allowed to play unless we found "other people like yourselves" to join our game. Whether it had something to do with our Jewish faith I can't be sure, but that certainly seemed to be the case. I can remember my father swearing that he would never go back there. Years later, after my father's death, I was invited to play there and, quite frankly, I was delighted to decline.

To my amazement, similar situations have taken place and still take place in banking halls of Wall Street. I'm sorry to say that there are certain houses, as there are certain golf clubs, which are still closed societies. The best thing to do is to aspire to greatness, on the course and in the office. One day, you can hope to have the opportunity to elect to dismiss those who once dismissed you.

PERSEVERANCE PAYS OFF

It was a cold May morning in San Francisco, which isn't exactly uncommon weather in the City by the Bay. I was on my home course, Lake Merced, and we were out by the ocean in the middle of a fog. I had bogeyed the first hole, and coupled with the depressing fog, was ready to walk off the course and call it a day. I decided to stick it out, and ended up birdying eight of the remaining 17 holes and shot a seven under 65, tying the Merced record set by our pro, Woody Wright.

By analogy, there is the story of a young college student who had a terrific idea for a business—an idea so fabulous it became the subject of his term paper at Yale University. The concept was to save the Federal Reserve System $3 million per day in float fees by flying Federal Reserve cash from region to region. His professor thought otherwise, and provided a litany of reasons why it would fail: There were too many obstacles, too many regulations, too many logistical problems to overcome and, finally, there was too much competition. The student received a "C" on his paper.

Undaunted by the lackluster grade, the student embarked on a wild journey in an effort to turn his dream into a reality. After prolonged discussions with the Federal Reserve System, he found himself on the verge of proving his nay-sayers wrong. Negotiations progressed successfully to the point where he put his entire $8.5 million inheritance on the line. He made major commitments to Pan Am for airplanes. He personally invested $250,000. He acquired a passenger plane to be modified for package delivery, and he guaranteed a $3.6 million bank loan. Then disaster struck! The Federal Reserve System elected not to pursue the program.

On the verge of personal financial ruin, the young man retooled his business plan, spent thousands of dollars on market studies, and successfully romanced the venture capital community. As a result, overnight shipping giant Federal Express was born!

As we've been told so many times, it isn't how you start that's important, it's how you finish.

THE GLOBAL GAME

I played in eight British Amateurs from 1989 through 1996, and they were the greatest experiences of my career. The level of golf in Britain and throughout the rest of Europe is as high as that in the United States, if not higher. That's not only because the Brits hold golf in higher regard, but also, because shot-making remains an art on the other side of the Atlantic. In the United States, if you can hit the ball long and straight, you're in good shape. But in Europe, courses are designed differently and conditioned differently. Some were built in the days of "penal" design, with bunkers in the middle of the fairways and trouble behind the greens, not in front. Because the greens don't hold the same, you have to think through each shot carefully, and maybe use a club or two less than you would for a similar distance on a U.S. course.

Doing business in a foreign country is no different, especially today, when businesses, small and large, are jumping at every opportunity to increase their sales by entering foreign markets. Even though golf is still golf, there are strategies and nuances to learn. As Peter Drucker said of the challenges Americans face when doing business with Japan, "No one in this country understands the Japanese situation. Yes, there are tremendous barriers in Japan, but they are not economic. They are social."

It's just as exciting to play golf in another country as it is to do business there. In 1996, with my British Amateur exemption coming to a close, I was determined to bring home more than just a memory from Turnberry. As part of the last group off the tee in the second day of qualifying, we weathered 50-mile-per-hour winds and torrential rains as we came to the 14th hole. Because nobody was around, I pried the flag off the stick and tucked it under my sweater. One of my partners, a young Englishman named Paul Casey, stared at me in disbelief. At the 16th green, an official of the Royal and Ancient, which controls the British Amateur, asked if anybody had seen the flag. Here I was, a 51-year-old San Francisco business executive, acting like a young teenager. And Casey, soon to be coming to the United States to play golf at Arizona State University, smiled and rubbed his hands together as if saying, "For money, I won't tell."

A year later Paul Casey came into my office, and there on the conference room wall was the Turnberry flag. When I look at it or talk about it, I remember the powerful wind and the exhilarating golf, and I'm reminded of the tremendous opportunities that lie outside the borders of the United States.

SUCCESS IS FLEETING

"What happened to Ian Baker-Finch?" is one of the great questions in golf. He was on top of the world after winning the 1991 British Open at Royal Birkdale. A champion and all-around good guy who the media referred to as "tall, dark, and hyphenated," he smiled a lot and was always in demand. And then, just like that, he lost the touch. Some said it was because he changed his swing to get more distance. Whatever the case, he went through the 1995 and 1996 PGA Tours without making more than one or two cuts. And in the 1995 British Open at St. Andrews, he missed the 100-yard wide fairway formed by the parallel 1st and 18th holes, starting with an out-of-bounds tee shot, left!

Every golfer has gone into a slump, including Palmer, Nicklaus, Watson, Trevino, and Miller. Some have had slumps that lasted for a year or two, but few have suffered the agony and mysterious misfortune of Baker-Finch. Still, it happens to everyone to some degree. You lose your swing and, worse yet, you lose your confidence. What came easily, especially when you were a teenager, suddenly doesn't come at all, even with hours of practice.

Success in business can be as fleeting as success in golf. When the market crashed in '87, many multimillionaires went bankrupt. Of course, enjoying success does not mean flaunting it. Instead, it means recognizing your achievements and understanding how they came about. And should your success prove to be temporary, it will still be a great source of self-confidence.

CONCLUSION: THE MAGIC OF GOLF

I enjoy golf, not only because no two courses are alike or because the scenery is always different and challenging, but also because of the wonderful people I meet.

You'll find that after four to five hours on a course, you will know just about everything you want to know about most of your companions. For that reason, I view golf as a terrific business tool, although discussing business while playing is something all executive golfers should try to avoid. The round of golf itself should be a rewarding experience for all parties concerned. If I'm playing with a prospective customer who wants my opinions on the market, I'll tell him, "We'll talk about it after the round." If I'm playing with a chief executive, I will listen to his opinions on business, but I won't ruin a day by getting into specifics. Mark Twain said "Golf is a long walk spoiled." But that's only if you allow it to be, by defeating the very purpose of the game—which is recreation and revitalization.

While golf can be used as a business vehicle, the game is much more than a creative networking method. David Forgan said "Golf is a test of character." It certainly is, and beyond that, it gives us great insight into the inner workings of the minds and souls of our golfing companions. By gauging our companions'—and our own—reactions to the sometimes unpredictable intricacies of the sport, we are in a much better position to decide whether those in whom we invest our time over a game of golf are also those in whom we should invest our money and our trust.